Mental Models

The Super Guide to Improve Decision Making,
Problem Solving and Logical Analysis.

Advanced Learning Guide to Critical Thinking.

The Art of Clear Thinking.

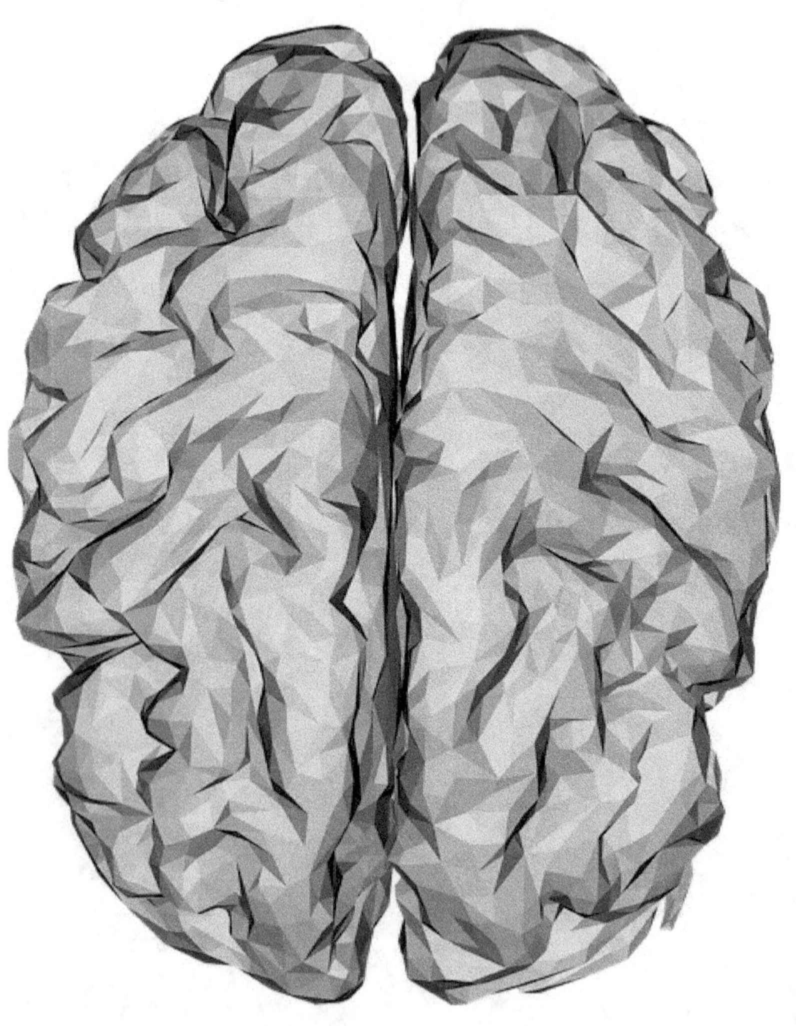

Table of Contents

original author of this work can be in any fashion deemed liable for any hardship or damages that may befall them after undertaking information described herein.

Additionally, the information in the following pages is intended only for informational purposes and should thus be thought of as universal. As befitting its nature, it is presented without assurance regarding its prolonged validity or interim quality. Trademarks that are mentioned are done without written consent and can in no way be considered an endorsement from the trademark holder.

Introduction

"Two heads are better than one," many people say. It's no surprise because our own biases and experiences limit us. We also lack the areas of expertise, which results in the development and priority of mental models that you might not realize in the first place.

For example, there are two employees. The first one excels in sales while the latter remains superb in other business aspects. When both of them work together, their combined insights can crack a challenge. However, it's not always possible to host a discussion when making a crucial decision. As a professional, it's important to think about the problem yourself. But the good news is that there's an excellent way to maximize your decision-making, commonly called mental models.

You probably have heard it before. But what is a mental model? How can you navigate your mental model? Good questions. You have come to the right place! In this eBook, you will know everything about mental modes! Are you ready? Take a close look at the following.

Chapter 1: Introduction to Mental Models

Known as an explanation of how something works, a mental model is considered an overarching term for framework, concept, or worldview. Called as a representation of the surrounding world, a mental model tells about the relationship between its parts and an individual's perception of his actions and consequences.

Mental models can help everyone understand life. The supply and demand, for example, is a mental model that supports individuals to elucidate and comprehend how the economy works. Game theory is also a mental model that enables a person to understand trust and relationship.

Mental models serve as a guide to one's behavior or perception. They act as a thinking tool that a person uses to make decisions, solve daily problems, and understand life as a whole. That's why learning a new model gives everyone the chance to perceive the world differently.

Despite intensive development, mental models remain imperfect but useful. A mental model in engineering or physics, for instance, doesn't provide an error-free explanation of the universe. However, the best mental methods from such disciplines have enabled professionals and other experts to build high-end bridges, develop innovative technologies, explore the outer space, and many more. *"Scientists agree that there's no 100% correct theory,"* according to historian Yuval Noah Harari. *"The test of knowledge is about utility. It goes beyond the truth,"* he added.

The best mental models are the ideas that a person employs the most. In general, they are useful in everyday living, and a clearer understanding will help someone to take good actions and make smart decisions. That's why developing and growing a base of mental models can play a critical role in rational and effective thinking.

As with a personal algorithm, mental models can help set an approach to handling and addressing a problem. They can also shape one's behavior, enabling a person to live life to the fullest. They can even play a big role in reasoning, cognition, and decision-making. *"The mind is able to build small-scale models to anticipate and deal with new events,"* Kenneth Craik said.

Experts believed that mental models have originated with Kenneth Craik's The Nature of Explanation in 1943. Published in 1927, Georges-Henri Luquet argued that a child could build internal models and the view has relatively influenced a number of psychologists, including Jean Piaget.

In 1983, Philip Johnson-Laird also published a book about mental models. In the same year, Albert Stevens and Deidre Gentner edited different chapters in a book entitled Mental Models.

Since then, the use of the idea in several fields has been prevalent, and Donald Norman is one of the researchers. The term situation model was first used by Teun A. van Dijk and Walter Kinstsch, and wherein they showed the importance of the thinking tools for discourse production and comprehension.

Chapter 2: How to Have Clear Thinking?

Called as a reasoning unclouded by prejudices and fears, clear thinking means accepted facts or assumptions. It is considered the ability to think critically or engage reflectively. An individual who has a good memory or can accumulate information is not a clear thinker.

Clear thinking is the capacity to deduce consequences and use the information to address a problem. It helps us acquire new knowledge and make smart life decisions. Clear thinkers can understand the connections between various ideas. They can determine, create, and assess arguments. They can detect inconsistencies in reasoning, address problems systematically, ascertain the relevance of ideas, perceive the world accurately, hypothesize, and reflect on their beliefs.

Clear thinking also plays a critical role in everyone's longevity or lifestyle. The clearer our thought, the better will be our capacity to perceive, put an end to everyday challenges, and become self-aware. The skill translates into wiser decisions regarding a person's personal achievements, interpersonal relationships, and purpose. More than that, clear thinking improves our contributions in the workplace and society as a whole. It also improves lifestyle and longevity.

However, different factors affect clear thinking. A place, for instance, can extremely influence your mind.

Time is also a big factor. The food you take, the past impressions, and actions can impact a person's way of thinking. So, how to have clear thinking? Remember that the clarity of thinking is not instant. It's a long and stressful process. It does not happen overnight. As time passes by, an individual can foster his mind, increasing efficiency and productivity.

To develop clear thinking, there are many helpful ways to follow. But the following list is the most acceptable and common steps to take into consideration. Read on for more information!

Check one's Attitude

It cannot be denied that focus follows an individual's desires. A person can think of new ideas and ways when he wants to achieve a goal in the first place.

On the other hand, a professional only think of reasons why it is not a perfect idea to pursue his goals when he lacks passion. To attain clear thinking, be honest about your desire. Do you want it? Do you do it because it's what you enjoy the most? Whatever the case may be, it will save your time at the beginning of all your pursuits.

Be Clear With Your Purpose

As with other goals, you have to be specific to achieve clear thinking. Sometimes, we may keep changing our objectives, which in turn can demand our brain to change its concentration and lose our path. To keep anyone's focus, sit for a minute or two, and write down. Think about what you want to achieve and stick to it. It's normal to get distracted in the midst of your journey. Just reflect on your purpose because it helps.

Take Advantage of Your Passion for managing Emotions

As you strive to turn clear thinking into a reality, your desire overcomes the challenges. However, these problems can overwhelm your emotions. This is especially true when a person suffers from a recent, potential loss.

To keep one's focus, look ahead to make your dreams a reality. Also, use your passion to control or manage your emotions.

Use Negative Thinking to Make a Smart Decision and a Positive Action

Negative thinking leads to a terrible negativity. It frees an individual's imagination to achieve what he wants in the beginning.

But negative thinking can also be an advantage. To produce a positive action, take advantage of the *'Why not = How to'* technique.

For example, you are unable to make a bright decision, solve the problem systematically, or evaluate arguments.

Many would see these weaknesses negatively. Of course, you would feel the same thing at first. But use them as a signpost to plan to reach your dreams.

To make a smart decision or handle a problem well, connect and weigh different ideas in mind. Reflect on your own values and beliefs. Detect the top mistakes in your reasoning. Plus, determine the importance of an idea. But you cannot do it on your own sometimes. Seek assistance from a colleague, friend, or family.

Use your Logic in Important Situations

Many of us can start with a clear focus. But we may be diverted by others, which in turn can affect our direction. To retain clear concentration and thinking, focus on the issue, and see the difference in every conversation. Don't just concentrate on the ego itself.

What does it mean? Or how does it work? In all conversations, make sure to concentrate on the issue you want to achieve. Don't direct your attention on your egos to reach your goal objectively.

Chapter 3: Importance of Critical Thinking Skills

As you master critical thinking skills, learn to understand logical connections between ideas, identify mistakes in reasoning, solve problems systematically or hypothesize, there's a multitude of benefits you can reap. The most common is to make a better decision. When you face a predicament about life's purpose, interpersonal relationships, or personal achievement, you can make a smart decision.

Here are the other importance of critical thinking skills:

It Develops or Encourages Curiosity

Curiosity stands beyond a profound understanding of what surrounds us. But it encourages us to go out of our comfort zone and seek other information to hone our skillset over time. A teacher, for example, looks for something new to provide effective, timely, and fun instruction.

Critical thinkers remain inquisitive about a variety of topics and have wide interests. They remain curious about the world and the people. Aside from the understanding, they have an appreciation for other people's beliefs, views, or cultures, which makes them a lifelong learner.

Since they are curious by nature, they apply clear thinking skills every moment. They are alert for an opportunity to apply their thinking habits in different situations. The desire to think of the simplest issues clearly can show their interests to receive constructive results.

Critical or clear thinkers always ask the following questions:

- Why is it necessary? Who is the affected part of the community?
- Is there something I overlook? What's hidden?
- Why should I listen to this professional? What learning can I acquire?
- What else should I take into consideration?

Critical thinkers don't stop asking questions. They enjoy exploring each side of a specific issue instead. They also love to elucidate deeper facts in all available data.

It Fosters Creativity or Imagination

Below problem solving, creativity is the second top skill that every child should learn, according to educators. It's no surprise because effective critical thinkers are largely creative individuals and creativity has defined itself as an essential skill in the modern workforce.

Clear thinking in marketing and business relies on a person's ability to be creative. When companies get the most out of their creativity throughout product development, they can stand out from the competition and succeed in the marketplace.

Creative people also question assumptions about different things. Rather than arguing for limitations, they ask *"why not"* or *"how?"* called eternal, which indicates that every individual is unlimited. What's surprising is that they don't get stuck in their comfort zone. They go out that comforting cocoon to learn new things, develop skills, unleash new capabilities, and become a versatile professional over time.

It Develops and Strengthens Problem-Solving Ability

Do you know that critical thinker are likely to be problem-solvers? Yes, it's a fact, and it's the most important skill that every learner should have in order to face future challenges and come up with imaginative solutions.

Albert Einstein, one of the most prolific investors, said that he's not so smart: it's just that he stayed with a problem longer. When given an hour to address a problem, he'd spend 5 minutes on the solution and the rest for research purposes. This kind of commitment and patience indicates the quality of what an effective critical thinker is. This is the reason why a critical thinking ability can play a big role in becoming a good problem solver.

Developing a clear and critical thinking ability prepares everyone to face complex predicaments in the coming years.

Whether it's global warming, overpopulation, pollution, energy crises, electronic waste management or water shortages, critical thinkers can produce lasting and innovative solutions to alleviate or put an end to these never-ending issues.

It's Considered a Multi-Faceted Practice

Known for encompassing a range of disciplines, critical thinking can cultivate a wide array of cognitive talents. It's indeed a cross-curricular activity for the mind, which must be exercised to function at its best.

Critical thinking promotes the development of other skills. These can include analytical thinking, reasoning skills, evaluative skills, planning skills, logical thinking, open-mindedness, observational skills, self-reflective capacity, language skills, decision making, questioning ability, creative visualization strategies, and more.

It Develops Independence

One of the primary goals of education is to train young students to think independently. When they start to think for themselves, they become independent, responsible, and ready to adjust in the modern and fast-paced industry.

Independent thinking skills are usually at the forefront of learning how to be a great thinker and effective leader. Independent thinkers learn how to make sense of what surrounds them based on observation and personal experience. In most cases, they can make critical and well-informed decisions, gain confidence, and learn from mistakes.

When individuals think critically, they do it in a self-directed manner. While the style of thinking is disciplined, it becomes a great self-correcting mindset. As they continue to develop the skills thru experience, the abilities can become second nature.

As stated earlier, independent thinking skills are among the competencies all educators strive to inculcate in every young student's mind. They do that to provide learners a gift they can use for a lifetime. Once they graduate, they can pursue their dreams with pride and confidence.

It's a Lifelong Skill

Lower order thinking skills prepare a student for today. Critical thinking and other higher-order competencies, on the contrary, prepare everyone for long-term success as they can adjust in a different setting outside the walls of the classroom. They can handle a range of situations in the workplace, finish their job well, become productive, and acquire a lucrative career. Although it is a long process to achieve these thinking abilities, the efforts are worth it.

It Plays a Vital Role in the New Knowledge-Economy

The new knowledge economy is driven by IT. Every professional need to deal with the everyday changes, and the economy places high demands on the competency to analyze information and incorporate sources of knowledge to solve problems. Superb critical thinking promotes such skills, which can come into play in this fast-paced workplace.

It Enhances Language Skills

Clear thinking can improve the way you express your ideas. Every time you face a group of people for a presentation, you will be as eloquent and accurate as possible. In analyzing the logical structure of texts and other relevant pieces of information, critical thinking can boost comprehension abilities, which can save your time and maximize results.

It is Crucial for Self-Reflection

To structure a meaningful life according to your desires, justifying and reflecting on your values, decisions, and beliefs can make a huge difference. To do that, critical thinking serves as a perfect tool for self-evaluation, especially during a failure or even success. Do you miss something important? What would you do to realize your goals? Ask these questions when you self-reflect.

It Enhances Academic Performance

"Students who know how to critique or analyze ideas can make connections across several disciplines. They can see knowledge as applicable to everyday living and understand any type of content on a longer-lasting and more profound level," Richard Paul and Linda Elder, Authors of Critical

Thinking Development: A Stage Theory said. This ability could help people of all ages to understand or fix a problem, which in turn can ensure a great academic performance or productivity. Without enough critical thinking skills, a person would find it hard to analyze his surrounding world, which can result in slow performance.

It Increases Awareness Between a Rational Thought and an Emotional Response

Knowing the difference between an emotional response and a rational thought is difficult. A critical thinker, on the other hand, makes it easy and simple. Through personal bias and careful consideration, they know how the former differs from the latter.

Emotion is considered the foe of reason. By understanding your perspective, you can consider other's point of view. Then, you can make a conclusion according to facts, not feelings.

It Guarantees a Great Hiring Opportunity

Nowadays, the number of employers who look for professionals with good thinking skills has been skyrocketing. It's no wonder because they can learn quickly, solve daily problems, analyze information, and think creatively. Although those with specialized academic skills sound in-demand, a critical thinker always has the edge over the other applicants.

It can be a Deciding Factor for a Promotion

Most high-paying jobs, these days, require higher-order thinking skills, which can include generating effective ideas and making smart decisions. More often than not, job interviewers ask applicants with questions that examine and test their ability. When seeking a promotion, these competencies will be of great help.

It Makes One's Approach

With critical thinking skills, critical thinkers are aware of different approaches on how to solve a problem. They can evaluate each approach critically. Instead of depending on a standard problem-solving method. They identify other valuable and effective techniques to increase productivity and success.

It Saves Time

As a critical thinker, you're certain that not all information is relevant to your problem-solving and decision making. However, some don't know how to get rid of any irrelevant data. Critical thinking skills teach you how to prioritize both of your resources and time. Then, you can analyze and assess what is important to the process, which helps you know whether or not a decision is a good one.

It Leads to Autonomous Learning

Instead of relying on teachers, students with a high level of critical thinking become self-directed and independent learners. Critical thinking skills allow students to evaluate their learning styles, weaknesses, and strength. These also enable them to take ownership or be responsible for their education. Students in an English class, for example, might write a reflective essay about how their writing skills have improved and what they need to focus on. This allows them to view their performance and reach good conclusions.

From solving problems in school to facing real-life situations, critical thinking skills enable the youth and professionals to present their ideas well. Instead of accepting their personal reasoning, they make a research, look for statistics, and other important data to prove their stance. Clear thinking can also result in empathy for other people's point of view and better control of one's learning.

It Brings New Ideas

When a potential issue exists in the workplace, many would assume that it falls under a predetermined category. Some who possess superb critical thinking don't make assumptions. Using their logical skills, they remove the temptation to classify a problem under a common problem in the past. Then, it forces managers and employees to look beyond traditional solutions and new ideas to address a predicament and achieve meaningful results.

It Promotes Other Options

Another advantage of critical thinking is that it enables a company to develop a variety of realistic and feasible solutions to address an issue. This allows businesses of all sizes to provide various solutions to prospective clients, and it also leads to effective innovation. With different solutions to a specific problem, a company can address a dilemma with the use of existing resources, saving their time, effort, and cash as well.

Chapter 4: What is Your Mental Model?

There are many mental models that people use every day, in which they don't realize in the first place. When we interpret the world or understand the relationship between things, our mental models come into play. When we face new life experiences or a problem, these thinking tools can make a critical role.

As we're born, we already have a mental model. As the years pass by, it becomes effectively strong and stable. Then, our mind unleashes or designs another mental model. As we learn and acquire experiences, our base of mental models becomes broader, which in turn can enable us to think clearly and rationally.

The world is, no doubt a complicated place, and trying to understand it leads to confusion. More than that, individuals learn to accept their limitations. While these can be a disadvantage, they provide professionals with opportunities to strengthen their weaknesses, foster strengths, become a critical thinker, and turn a high level Yof performance into a reality.

You probably are wondering what your mental models are. While some are considered common knowledge, others are sophisticated, and the latticework they produce is intimidating to deal with. Don't worry! You're not alone! Most beginners and even seasoned critical thinkers experience the same thing.

The most common mental model is Murphy's Law. Known as an optimistic law, the metal model states that if anything can go wrong, it surely will. Murphy's Law also indicates that if there are two ways to do something, and one of them can lead to a big mess, a person will still do it. But its explosive nature is the idea that someone will make the wrong choice whatever his decisions to take.

Occam razor is another mental model to know. Although it's difficult as it sounds, it states that the simplest explanation is the correct one. When a person tries to understand what really happened, the development of the most basic hypothesis can help.

Hanlon's razor is another common mental model that we might have. What does it mean? And how does it work? A marketing qualified lead, for example, goes dark at some point during the acquisition process. Then, you might assume that the client doesn't want to continue.

However, Hanlon's Razor asks everyone not to attribute to malice what could be explained by carelessness. Instead, it's realistic to assume that the person has a hectic schedule.

Pareto principle, on the other hand, is commonly called as the 80/20 rule, which means the results are not properly distributed. For instance, 20% of your time produces approximately 80% of the results and 20% of the work leads to 89% of the returns. If you can hone on the necessary skills, the success rate is higher than you have ever thought. But it's easier said than done. It is a long and stressful process, which requires one's patience, commitment, and persistence.

Another mental model is Sturgeon's law, which means 90% of everything is considered crap. That's why you have to be selective with both of your energy and time. How to begin? Start with the non-crap and then find your way out. While some are likely to rush, get the process done as slowly as possible. Unlike the Pareto Principle, it is a more restrictive version in most cases.

Last but not least is Parkinson Law. Compared to other mental models, it is quite different, which indicates that triviality can set in easily because it feels great to voice a person's opinion and feel productive. When your mental model is similar to Parkinson law, reflect on your top priorities. Then, ask if your actions are relevant to your goals. From there, work expands to fill your time and remember that working at a relaxed pace can result in self-sabotage.

To know more information about the common and popular mental models, read on! We discussed other thinking tools in detail in the succeeding chapters.

Chapter 5: How to be Open-Minded?

While mental models refer to the representation of the surrounding world, open-mindedness is about the ability of a person to adopt assumptions based on a changing circumstance at work or in other places. Since the working environment leads to new occurrences, individuals are unable to reach expectations and make the objectives happen.

The application of open-mindedness, however, makes the mind flexible to overcome a specific situation, which in turn can bring academic performance and productivity up to the highest level. How's it possible? Well, by changing the assumptions and adopting relevant suppositions, it could be a reality.

Unlike mental models, open-mindedness leads to the flexibility of the mind to adopt assumptions, which can enable them to solve existing challenges in their daily living. Because of the complexity of the 21st business environment, companies look for critical thinking and open-minded professional.

But how to be open-minded? As with mental models, acquiring quality takes time and attention; it also requires a lifelong process for someone to develop the in-demand skill in the workplace, studies, and another environment.

To be open-minded, everyone might find it tough because most of us set a certain comfort in our mind that's hard to break. However, opening the mind to new opportunities, adventure, relationships, and knowledge can bring a greater sense of happiness or fulfillment to your daily living.

Before anything else, find your motivation. For everyone to make it possible to embrace and accept new ideas, it's imperative to motivate oneself to try different things. Ask why do you want to become open-minded? Are you committed to accepting different assumptions from your colleagues and other people that surround you? Are you more than willing to take action to turn this goal into a reality? Then, you probably are ready.

After that, it's a perfect time to choose specific areas to develop. Which life areas do you want to open up to ideas? For example, if you're eating the same food all the time, you perhaps like to try some variation. You can give at least one recipe or food a shot every week. It's a realistic and simple approach, after all.

While many would aim high, don't do the same thing. Start from a small goal because you might not be ready to experience a sudden and big change in your life. That's why chunk your objectives into small pieces to make this approach reliable and realistic.

After finding your motivation and choosing the areas to develop, your job does not stop there. In fact, it's just the beginning of your journey towards becoming an open-minded individual. Before we learn how to become open-minded, below are some benefits of having an open mind:

Let Go of Control

Close-minded people don't grow personally and professionally. They believe they are higher than anyone else in terms of expertise, knowledge, and experience. But the truth is that they don't grow as a professional. Open-minded, on the other hand, individuals have the opportunity to be in control of their thoughts. They allow themselves to acquire new ideas and challenge their existing beliefs.

"Nothing permanent in this world but change," everyone says. Every second, the workplace, the school, and other places change. So, close-minded individuals are unable to adapt to new trends, making their knowledge obsolete. But the ability to accept assumptions, facts, or opinions enable them to be flexible and effective.

Experience Change

Opening up your mind to new thoughts gives you the chance to change how you perceive the world. But this doesn't mean it will change your existing beliefs and perspectives. Sometimes, the process may just strengthen your mental faculties, and open-mindedness allows you to achieve stronger outcomes and a fulfilling life.

More often than not, some are afraid to adapt the latest trends or innovation. It's no surprise because they are not ready to fail. They think that accepting other's ideas and failing make them incapable or ineffective. But we're not perfect after all. Some are good in math, while others are poor. Although you struggle with numbers, you may be good in other fields. So, consider the latest change or ideas as an opportunity to foster and become more competitive in the coming years. Take them seriously and find your own ways for personal and professional development.

When someone suggests an idea, don't feel negative about it. In fact, you can consider yourself lucky because a thought from peers and superiors can help you bridge the gap, identify a better solution, save your time, and maximize a perfect result at the end of the day.

Make Yourself Vulnerable

It's scary to discern the world thru an open mind because you show your vulnerability to others. You also admit that you lack in terms of knowledge and performance. The process can be exhilarating and confusing, as well.

But it's good to know that making yourself vulnerable can be a good thing. First, you will learn different things, develop your skills, meet expectations, and bring your knowledge up to the highest level. Second, the process becomes easier than expected while you get as competitive as possible. Last but not least is that your relationship with your colleagues, peers, and other people that surround you will be meaningful.

So, don't be skeptical to look vulnerable. With the help of others and your persistence to excellence, your weaknesses will surely be your strengths in the future. But don't heavily rely on colleagues. Remember that learning by doing is better, which in turn can lead to productivity, effectiveness, and flexibility.

Make Mistakes

Committing mistakes is embarrassing but a great learning experience. However, many professionals, business owners, or students don't grow after a failure and end up staying in their comfort zone. If you experience the same thing, you're not alone. Instead of lingering on a failure, consider it a learning experience for you to be a better version of yourself. What you need to do after a failure is to reflect. Did you overlook something important? What resources did you miss? From there, you'd realize why you make a mistake. Also, other people are more than willing to provide a constructive criticism. Although it hurts and affects your self-confidence, don't feel down because it's part of the process. As long as you exert effort to improve your weaknesses, you can handle the same problem easily and effectively.

Strengthen your Weaknesses

You probably are expert in communication skills, presentation, or language. Perhaps, you're poor in critical thinking activities. To strengthen yourself, being open-minded provides you a platform to acquire and build upon a base of ideas from reliable professionals. As years pass by, every thought you collect from others adds up. This strengthens your skills, enables you to acquire a new ability, and improves your limitations.

But remember that building on experiences is hard without an open mind. When you receive a feedback from superiors, take it as a constructive criticism. It hurts but looks at it positively. Also, it's essential to read in the library or online. For those who don't have ample time to go to the nearest library, turn on your phone and browse the internet with a click of a button.

Gain Confidence

Close-minded individuals are confined by their own beliefs or other's perspectives. Open-mindedness, on the contrary, enables you to have a strong sense of yourself. This means you can boost the level of your self-esteem. When you're in front of a big crowd, you can carry yourself well. For a presentation and other activities, you can perform according to your goals and other standards.

Close-minded people lack confidence. In fact, they stay in their comfort zone and believe that their knowledge is unmatched. But the truth is that most of their skills need improvement. For you to boost your self-esteem, start to be open-minded, and don't stop learning.

Be Honest As much As Possible

Close-minded people are not honest enough to admit that they lack the skills. Individuals with an open mind are different. At first, they admit that the level of their knowledge is far from perfection, and this understanding leads to a sense of authenticity. When you're honest with your capabilities, many would love to give you a hand, which can establish a good rapport in the long run. Whenever you go, you can build a fun relationship with others, establishing a fun and competitive working environment.

For some, being open-minded is as easy as eating a pie. For others, it's a real headache. It's something they need to think constantly and make an effort to obtain. However, thinking openly and embracing new ideas will produce benefits for both of your career and life.

Since you struggle to face the challenge, what are you going to do next? Here are what you can use or adapt to be open-minded in 2019 and beyond. Are you ready? Take a close look at the following:

Talk Less and Listen More

Before you can covey your real message, you have to seek first to understand. We don't specifically learn new things when we talk more. By listening intently and silently, we can acquire fresh ideas. When interacting with other people, listen profoundly for at least 70% of your time. Don't use your phone or stop multitasking. That way, you can focus and learn new ideas and approaches, which are a key for personal and professional development.

Avoid Snap Decisions

How many times has an event hit you straight directly in your blood pressure? Does the email go unreturned? Does a call go unanswered? Do you learn a bad surprise thru a memo or second party? Whatever the case may be, most of us react to an unexpected as immediately as possible. But is it a good idea? Well, making snap decisions is not a smart action. Instead of showing anger or judgment, get the facts first. Don't be deceived by your emotions. Control and gather everything you need. This can guarantee a good flow, promote a stress-free environment, and boost productivity.

Show your Earnest Gratitude to People's Suggestions

There are several causes of consternation in any settings. The lack of gratitude for an idea is among them. It's normal to feel a sense of injustice when colleagues steal a specific employee's ideas. But will they be likely to offer their critical thinking again? Of course, not. They will save their ideas for another company where they feel appreciated and respected for their job. As a colleague and professional, bear this courtesy in mind.

Encourage Frankness and Don't Be Afraid to Handle It

Have you ever received a straight and straightforward feedback? What did you feel? Did you feel hurt? Or were you unwillingly accepted what you have heard? Then, remember that sensitive feelings can relatively influence your performance in school, at home, or in the workplace. To reduce the impact, accept it. Then, start to take a criticism constructively.

When you meet someone who couldn't accept the truth regarding his performance, be wary when giving your feedback. Make sure to incorporate high tact and diplomacy. Respect for the person should be noticeable and obvious. If you master this ability, your skill to speak, hear, and share with an open mind will make the impossible possible.

Look for Other Opportunities

One of the results of being open-minded is the ability to seek or discover opportunities and approaches to addressing everyday challenges.

It's normal to think that there are no available ideas. But look at every possibility and angle to put an end to a problem.

Thomas Edison has earned worldwide popularity because of its lightbulb. But he had attempted a thousand times before he perfected his invention according to reports and studies.

Another inventor who had the same trait is Colonel Sanders, in which he tried his chicken recipe for approximately 1,009 times according to sources. When you learn to accept new opportunities, you will never get tired to make an effort to fulfill your dreams. If you feel hopeless, don't rush. Pause, think, and start again.

Chapter 6: Spend the Time Wisely

A good time management leads to more productivity. Professionals at home or in the office are able to get more things done compared to those who can't spend their time wisely. They have more energy for everything they need to fulfil. They feel less stressed and relate positively to everyone around them. They also feel better about themselves, enabling them to live life to the fullest and experience a deep sense of fulfillment.

However, managing or spending your time wisely is easier said than done. In fact, it depends on skills learned thru planning, self-control, evaluation, and self-analysis. Some strategies work best for you. But it depends on your level of discipline, personality, and ability to motivate yourself.

The mental model can also come into play. But what kind of mental model that can enable you to manage your time? This is where the Pareto Principle has got anyone's back. In chapter 4, we have learned that the mental model is known as the 80/20 rule. Used to analyze tasks or manage workload, the

Pareto Principle is one of the most useful techniques for spending time properly.

But how the 80/20 rule gives clarity to a person's life? Generally speaking, you can incorporate the principle into your personal life to alleviate inefficiency and maximize productivity. How are you going to do it? Let's get started!

- These days, let's accept the fact that we spend a lot of time using our phone. We always open one or more apps for entertainment and information. Well, it's a bad idea. Figure out the apps you use most of the time. Then, delete what's unnecessary. From there, you would see a big difference in the time you save and use for productive activities.

- In the workplace, imagine you are bombarded with different tasks every day. How are you going to deal with it? At first, it's overwhelming and tiring. But identify 20% of the tasks that are extremely important and make sure it brings 80% of the results. Having said that, you can manage or prioritize your daily activities in the office better. This helps you get the most of your time, reduces effort, and leads to good outcomes.

- Most of us like to wear the same clothes on a regular basis. It's about time to give your wardrobe a rest. Start from decluttering your closet by donating some of your unused dresses to charity to free up your mind as well.

- There's probably a number of video games and television shows that account for the 80% of your time. So, pick your top favorites and stop jumping from a game to another.

- It's estimated that approximately 80% of your money is spent on unnecessary things. Sometimes, you go to the mall without a list of stuff to buy. Also, other people get tempted to try things they are neither useful nor imperative. The secret here is to make a list, stick to it, and create a careful budget planning.

Applying the 80/20 Rule for Effective Time Management

Whether you're aiming to manage your time or set a goal, you can enjoy many benefits when you apply the mental model effectively. While some make big and drastic changes, don't do the same thing because it's unrealistic and impossible to achieve. Little changes in your habits or lifestyle are a good start.

If you are quite confused about how to apply the 80/20 rule, don't worry as here are some easy and quick tips to bear in mind:

Start and Finish the Hardest Tasks

There are different kinds of employees in the workforce. Some seem super-busy and work day and night without finishing every assigned and urgent task. Others finish everything ahead of time and look for other duties to handle.

Which of these best represents you as an employee? If you relate yourself to the former, don't lose hope or feel stressed with your situation. First, understand that the case happens when you do low-priority tasks. Look for something that will add real value to your work instead. Then, start with a complex task. Although it might consume most of your time, all your efforts will pay off at the end of the day. While it's tempting to do small and simple things, make the hardest activities a top priority.

Stick to Your Main Goal

What makes successful people different from others? Attitude comes first. When setting goals, they work on it despite the failures. When it comes to their time, they are likely to be intentional on how it is utilized. Even though it is tempting to indulge in gossips, side-talks, or distractions, they are focused. Then, they never lose track of their development and progress.

Of course, everyone wants to be successful and wealthy. So, what's the secret? Keep your eyes on your goal, use Pareto's principle, and don't lose hope despite the failures. Take them positively and exert more effort to manage your time and make your dreams happen.

Determine what Affects your Concentration

Staying focused on your task is hard, especially when there are distractions around you. You're not alone because most employees and even students find distractions the main roadblock to productivity. But some colleagues have their way out with distractions. So, if they can, you can do the same thing.

Of course, every item has a deadline, so getting distracted is something you cannot afford. To keep your focus, keep your phone on a silent mode to avoid the notification sounds and make your concentration stronger. Also, we are likely to get distracted by many things. The secret here is to determine what distracts you the most. Then, try your best to keep them away. At first, it's hard. But your efforts, time, and attention will all be worth it in the future.

Other Strategies for Better Time Management

Know-How You Spend your Time

It may sound unnecessary to determine how you spend your time every day. But it's relatively helpful. To do that, simply keep a log and record what you do for 15-minute intervals for a single week or two. Then, evaluate the outcomes. To assess the results, ascertain which tasks require most of your time and identify when you are most effective. Is it your job, recreation, family, or personal?

Identifying the most time-consuming activities can enable you to identify and create a customized action. In addition, that knowledge can assist you to be realistic and specific in planning. You can also estimate ample time for other important activities.

Be Sure to Set Priorities

Spending time wisely requires a distinction between what is urgent and what is important. Professionals agree that the most important paperwork is not the most urgent task to finish. But we are likely to let the urgent dominate our everyday routine at home or in the workplace.

While urgent and important tasks must be done, experts recommend that we should minimize our attention to projects that are not important despite their urgency. This allows you to keep your focus and achieve the results you desire. In addition, it enables you to control your time, maximize success, and reduce stress.

The simplest ways to prioritize is to create and develop a "to do" list. Whether you make a daily or weekly list, consider your lifestyle and rank all items in an order.

Take Advantage of a Planning Tool

Have you ever heard about personal planning tools? You can use them to boost your productivity. Good examples include pocket diaries, computer programs, calendars, index cards, electronic planners, and notebooks. Writing your tasks and schedules down can free your mind to concentrate on top of your priorities. If you are an auditory learner, you may find dictating your thoughts comfortable. To find the perfect tool, use the one that works for your situation.

Get Fully Organized

Disorganization leads to poor time management. That's why professional organizers suggest everyone remove the clutter. With unnecessary items, you may find decluttering complicated. You can set up three boxes labeled "Toss," "Keep," and "Give Away."

Discard items in the "Toss" box and include stuff in the "Give Away" box you'd like to sell. Plus, put the items you want to use in the "Keep" box. After decluttering, your job does not stop there. When the mess is gone, implement a system that enables you to handle less information.

Stop Procrastinating

Have you ever experienced putting off tasks because they seem overwhelming and confusing? You can break them down into smaller and feasible segments. When you're having a trouble on how to get started, collect materials, and organize notes. After that, build your own reward system whenever you complete a specific task.

Don't Attempt to Multi-Task

Multi-tasking can be an advantage but a problem as well. Every time you switch from one paperwork to another, you could lose your time, which can cause a loss of productivity. Recent studies show that multi-tasking does not save time. More than that, it can cause difficulties in keeping and maintaining your concentration.

Most importantly, the key to time management is discipline, commitment, patience, and persistence. Without all these qualities, you will always end up procrastinating and losing your focus.

Chapter 7: Gets Better Decision Making

The ability to make a good and quick decision is essential in different life situations. To be an effective employee or professional, decision-making skills can play a critical role. Whether you love a guessing game or don't believe in your instinct, you will lose the respect of the people that surround you. More than that, your decision may ruin your expected outcome.

An excellent decision making, on the contrary, can save you time. You know which decisions to make and the ones that require further research or careful planning. You can avoid overthinking, which can save you time. The skill can also foster respect. A well-informed and confident manager in a company, for example, can earn the trust of his employees as easily as possible.

A high level of decision-making skills can serve as motivation. A person who's superb in making decisions can serve as an inspiration to others to perform and achieve. In the workplace, not all of the days are a good one. Sometimes, there are moments where your colleagues struggle to do their job, and someone else who is good in decision making can change the atmosphere.

In addition, the capacity to decide on an important issue can also prevent a potential conflict and increase productivity. While a team works in a stress-free environment, they can become as competitive as possible.

However, getting a better decision making is not as simple as everyone thinks. In fact, it takes a long but fun process. However, as with effective time management, mental models can help an individual make an ideal option despite the level of difficulty. Occam's razor is among the mental models that can play a crucial role in acquiring and mastering decision-making skills. In the previous chapter, we have also learned that Occam's Razor shows that the simplest solutions are likely to be right. Or in a different case, a person makes a choice according to the least number of assumptions, and many find it useful when they don't have the data for a well-informed decision. In such situations, most of us take the path with minimum assumptions, which introduce an error. For those who design or develop a user flow for a product, the mental model comes in handy.

Compounding is another mental model that can make a difference in one's decision making. But how does it help in better decisions? It simply allows us to realize that if we continually make good habits, those will double in the long run and support us to reach our goals within a short period.

Oftentimes, we may forget that small efforts can lead to something monumental and compounding keep our focus. No matter how difficult our goal to fulfil, we would think of the best solution to realize our dreams.

Aside from mental models, there are other ways to get better decision making. The following is a short list of steps to incorporate into your existing approaches:

Make Decision Reversible

What're the best decisions? Many would think that collecting enough information can make good career choices. Well, it can be true. However, it may affect our progress. It can even pose a danger to our lives as well.

Most successful people adopt simple and flexible heuristics to get rid of the need for deliberation in specific situations. Jeff Bezos, the founder of Amazon, asks whether a decision is reversible or irreversible, making it one of the common and popular heuristics.

What is a reversible decision? Well, it happens when someone makes it fast despite the insufficiency of information. How about an irreversible decision? It indicates that an individual slows down the process. Not only do they understand the problem, but they also ensure to consider enough evidence on their hands.

Jeff Bezos took advantage of this heuristic to found the largest online shopping platform across the world. At first, he recognized that if his pursuit of success failed, he could be able to return to his job. His decision could be considered reversible, which served him well throughout the years. In fact, the heuristic continues to pay off when Bezos makes a decision.

Decisions amidst Uncertainty

Imagine you try to eat in a new restaurant after reading an online review. Although you haven't been there, are unaware of the food, or the atmosphere is stressful, you use the information to make a decision. You even recognize that it won't be a big deal when the restaurant doesn't meet your standards.

However, uncertainty is riskier in other situations. You might take a specific job without the knowledge of the company culture.

Reversible decisions are made as quickly as possible without gathering enough information. If your decision doesn't work out, you can extract wisdom from your experience with little cost. Oftentimes, gathering information, and looking for answers are not worth the time and attention. Even though extensive research and careful planning can make your decision better, the risk of missing a chance is higher than expected.

Reverse decisions should not be an excuse to be ill-informed or act recklessly. However, it is a belief that you should adapt. Unlike irreversible decisions, reversible ones are far different. You don't need to make it like the latter.

The skill to make fast decisions can give a person a great advantage. One benefit is that small-sized businesses can move with velocity while seasoned companies move with speed. What's the difference? It indicates the difference between a failure and success.

Let's say you are headed from New York to Las Vegas and just circle around NYC for hours. It shows that you're moving with speed. However, you're not getting to your desired destination. So, speed doesn't care whether you are reaching your objectives or not.

On the contrary, velocity is different. While speed doesn't give attention to the realization of your goals, velocity requires you to move toward your dreams. That's why startups and other small businesses make quick decisions to stand apart from the competition. You can also maximize the advantage with the pace of change and other factors. The quicker you react or respond, the better the benefit you can reap.

Every decision provides us with ample data to make better choices in the future. The faster we can cycle thru the OODA loop, the better the result. While many believe that the framework is only applicable to specific situations, it is a heuristic that can play an essential part in the decision-making the process.

With enough practice and careful planning, we can become expert in identifying bad decisions, including pivoting. Aside from avoiding to stick with past choices, we can stop viewing a failure as disastrous. Then, we can view them as information that will help us make good options in the future.

Jeff Bezos compares every reversible decision to doors, which open both ways. Irreversible decisions, on the other hand, are doors that enable passage in a single direction that can get you stuck if you walk thru.

Most decisions are the reversible ones, although we can't recover both the resources and time. Plus, the reversible door provides us enough information, making us aware of what's on the different side.

Malcolm Gladwell also explains why decision making in uncertainty can be effective in his book entitled *Blink: The Power of Thinking without Thinking*. Most of us assume that sufficient information results in a better life choice. A physician, for example, suggests extra tests. Of course, we are likely to believe that additional examinations can lead to a good outcome. However, Gladwell opposes the idea. *"Everyone has to know less information to determine the signature of a phenomenon. What we need is evidence of the blood pressure, an unstable angina, fluid in the lungs, or ECG,"* he said.

"In many areas of medicine, more information does not necessarily improve the outcomes. As an example, Gladwell cites a man who arrives at a hospital with chest pains. While his vital signs don't indicate any risk factors, his lifestyle is a different case. Two years earlier, he had a serious heart operation. When the attending physician considers all available data, it seems that the person should be admitted to the hospital. Plus, the other factors are not necessary in the short term run, but he is probably at a high risk of having a cardiovascular disease over time," Gladwell added.

When you're on the lookout for a heuristic for the development of your decision making, Bezos' approach is a good strategy to use in your career and life situations. What makes his heuristic different from others is that it fights the stasis in small-sized companies and even large organizations. What matters the most is that it's effective. Although it doesn't adhere to the norm of a slow decision, Bezos' technique proves that everything is possible in making a reversible choice.

Seek Satisfaction

Another way to get better decisions is to seek satisfaction. Mostly, we get satisfied with our decisions by the process or the decision itself. Is it of high quality? Does it lead to the attainment of your goals? Does it help you get nearer in your dreams? Whatever the case may be, satisfaction in your life choices can result in a better decision making in the future.

Emotions trigger how a person feels and behaves. When you're satisfied and happy with the past decisions, you can handle the same situation with a perfect choice. What will happen when you're sad and not content with your recent performance? Well, you might be willing to settle for things that don't reach your favor in the first place. When everything seems chaotic, various questions will come to your mind. Why did you make such a hasty and unplanned decision? What did you do wrong and overlook? But think again. Everything is done, and you could not travel back in time.

More than the nature of a decision, emotions can relatively affect the speed at which you make a choice. Anger can cause a rash and poor decision-making. The deep level of excitement is no exception. When you're excited, you could make decisions without weighing the implications in mind. If you feel afraid, your life choices may be filled with uncertainty, which in turn can take you longer to pick.

In addition to logic, emotion can play a critical role in helping us make good choices. Whether we understand our emotions and notice how they impact our thinking, we can manage our response and practice better options. Also, raise your logic while decreasing the emotional reactivity. You can list the pros and cons of every complicated decision because seeing every fact on a sheet of paper can aid you to think rationally about your choices. Furthermore, you can prevent emotions from enabling you to find a better version of yourself.

Don't feel Afraid and Negative on the Consequences

A person's decision entails predicting the future. In most cases, we visualize how the results of our options will make us feel and plump for the decision that can make us happy at the end of the day.

While this effective forecasting is fine, most of us can't get the most out of it. Most particularly, we tend to overestimate the effect of life events and the results of our decision. We always think that winning the lottery will make us more contented than it will in reality. *"The consequences of such events are less intense and shorter than we think,"* Daniel Gilbert, a psychologist from Harvard University, said.

What factor that leads us to come up with bad predictions? Well, the loss of aversion is the major factor. What does it mean? It's the belief that a failure will hurt more than the learning itself. Many individuals are unwilling to do a 50:50 bet except when the price is twice the amount they might lose according to Daniel Kahneman, a psychologist from Princeton University. Gilbert, together with his colleagues, shows that when people lose, they found it less painful than they have expected.

Then, Gilbert puts it down to a person's ability to rationalize every situation. *"Everyone can find new ways to see and make the world a much better place to dwell in,"* he also added.

So, what does a poor affective forecaster mean? Instead of imagining how a result might be stressful at the end of the day, look for a friend, colleague, and other peers who made the same life choice and know how they felt. Also, bear in mind that whatever your future is, it may please or hurt you. But don't play it safe. Although the failure is less risky than you think, it won't allow you to grow. It's best to commit mistakes because it becomes a great learning experience for people of all ages. Plus, don't be afraid of the consequences. Take them lightly, learn from your blunders, and become a much better professional.

Find out What Your Heart Desires

Success comes from determining your desired result. For you to fulfill your goal, you need holistic concentration. Despite the challenges along the way, don't lose sight of your specific targets.

When making choices, ask whether it is getting you closer to your objectives or it is getting you far away from your dreams. When it doesn't help you at all to make your goals happen, discard it as soon as possible. In addition, work on both of your mindset and beliefs to approach your target more effectively. While others may have failed on the same path because of weak thoughts, don't be swayed by the limitations others throw on you. Remember that a weak mind leads to poor results. Also, don't forget that attitude or winning is an option.

Establish an Effective Filter System

Does your decision only benefit yourself? Does it positively impact your family? Does it help your growth plans? Does it give other people an advantage? Whether a life choice or decision meets all these factors, you can make the perfect action, although the process is less attractive or longer.

When you don't use a filter, incorporate one approach to make good choices. After that, stick to them, whatever happens. When everything doesn't exceed your expectations, it's perhaps not ideal action.

Develop Wisdom

Every right decision always brings a good job, profound satisfaction, a lucrative career, and other rewards. How about bad life choices? Well, it still has a reward to reap. The experience itself is a good learning opportunity.

However, you can transform your daily experiences into wisdom. Just dig into your past bad options and understand what you can do in a different manner, which takes humility.

Wisdom also gives you the chance to identify the difference between reversible and irreversible decisions. Then, you can permit yourself to make well-informed and bold risks. You can also make mistakes without any fear or hesitations. Whenever you commit simple or complex blunders, you can take them as constructive criticism for your professional and personal development.

Fear of failure has been associated with conservative and slow decision. Poor life choices can even affect the quality of your thoughts. Instead of feeling afraid to commit mistakes, you should have at least tried. What if something great happened? When the result is not what you expected in the first place, it's still a perfect way to grow as a professional.

Let's say you have a new and fresh idea for an upcoming event in the company or organization you're currently working. Imagine your colleagues or superiors reject your idea. So, what will happen next? While some would feel hopeless, it's better to improve on your thought, make a research, and offer it to other businesses.

If the result is the same, reflect again. Do you think you overlook something important? Study and develop your ideas. Even you fail a thousand times, keep your sight in reaching all your dreams. Although you are lost in the midst of your journey, visualize your objectives.

Keep your Overconfidence in Check

Do you know that overconfidence can make your judgment and reasoning awry? Recent studies and research indicate that people are likely to overestimate the accuracy of their knowledge and their performance.

Perhaps, you are 90% certain you can convince your superiors to promote you. Or maybe, you are 100% sure you know your ideas can lead to huge business success. If you're overconfident about such things, your plans will go awry.

It's imperative to consider the level of your confidence when it comes to time management. Many of us tend to overestimate how much we can achieve within a short period of time. Do you think finishing your report will only take an hour or two? Do you believe that you can pay your bills within a few minutes? You might be overconfident in all your predictions.

Before anything else, spend time to estimate the chance of your success rate. Then, review and examine your estimates. Ask if your thought is as accurate as you imagined. Remember that good decision maker and critical thinkers recognize in their lives that overconfidence could be a big predicament. Then, adjust your behavior and way of thinking.

Identify Every Risk You Take

Familiarity always leads to comfort, and it's risky to make poor decisions. It's because you probably are accustomed to your weak habits. You even don't think about all the dangers along the way.

For example, you might drive at a high speed to come to your destination before your shift starts. Let's say you always arrive in the office without a traffic or ticket violation. As time passes by, you get more comfortable with fast driving. However, the truth is that you jeopardize your safety, and you take a legal risk.

Another good example is when you eat fast food every day. Since you don't see signs of serious complications, you might not consider it a big problem. But you may experience health issues or gain weight in the long run.

The secret here is to determine the habits that you become accustomed to. Why? It's because these are the things that require your attention. After that, assess whether your decisions are unhealthy or harmful. Then, create and develop a plan to have good habits.

Chapter 8: How to See More Clearly?

Clear thinking is not something that many people instinctually do. It cannot be denied that humans look for pleasure, food, survival, and sex. Everything else that a person views as a higher pursuit is only second. This is where mental models can come into play, ensuring that we think clearly and critically. Bear in mind that the world looks different at a second or third glance.

Clear thinking sounds simple to achieve. But the truth is that it is easier said than done and mental models make everything less stressful and more challenging. In the previous chapters, we have learned that mental models can help an individual make better decision making. Clear thinking is no exception.

To perceive the world as accurately as possible and think at your best, there are various things to do or consider. At first, it's confusing where to start, and neophytes have a higher risk to fail. But it doesn't necessarily mean that experienced individuals can handle the process effectively. People of all ages would have a hard time to think clearly and critically.

In this chapter, we will learn how to see more clearly to help us face our daily challenges well and avoid stressful consequences over time. Are you ready? Let's get started!

Ignore Black Swan

The first thing to think clearly is to ignore black swans. You probably have heard of black swans before. But what does it mean? How does it work? And what makes ignoring black swans beneficial?

A black swan is simple and unpredictable event, which has severe consequences and is beyond what you expect in the first place. A black swan event is characterized by its rarity, impact, and the practice of explaining a failure.

A black swan is considered a rare event with serious results. Although many people claim it to be predictable, others say that it cannot be predicted in advance. Any black swan events can even result in catastrophic effect to a specific economy. Since they are not predictable, it's possible to be prepared by building strong and effective systems. Of course, most of us will rely on forecasting tools. But the truth is that the use of such solutions can fail to predict and boost vulnerability to black swans. More particularly, it can increase risk and provide inefficient security.

Black Swan was popularized or coined by Nassim Nicholas Taleb who is a finance professor, former Wall Street trader, and writer. Prior to the 2008 financial crisis, Taleb wrote the black swan event in 2007. *"Since a black swan event is impossible to foresee because of its catastrophic consequences and extreme rarity, people need to assume that it's always possible. Then, extensive research and a careful planning can play a critical role,"* he argued.

For rare events, the tools of prediction and probability don't apply because they depend on the past sample sizes and large population. Extrapolating based on observations of past events is not useful as well. It can even pose a potential risk to us.

Nowadays, the experienced team ignores the early signs of black swans. Then, they move forward into their goals despite the problems. Why do you think individuals ignore a black swan event? It's because it can help clear their minds, materialize an event, and prepare them for a chaotic problem in the coming years.

Look for Equilibrium Point

Another mental model to see more clearly is to look for an equilibrium point. For the past years, the number of ways to visualize the concept has been skyrocketing. But the one that comes from Boombustology is the simplest and the most effective solution to use. How does it work? Or what makes it different from others? Well, it's where a ball sits on a curved shape.

Equilibrium is possible when the ball itself find its unique location. This is especially true when it's left to its devices. Overshooting and undershooting the location can be self-correcting. Disequilibrium, on the contrary, happens when the ball cannot find its location. That's not all! The ball cannot generate a self-correcting move. Disequilibrium can generate self-reinforcing motion, which accelerates the ball's move away from such a stable state.

Equilibrium is also considered a balance between opposing forces. Just like the variety of mental models, there are various types of equilibrium as well. You probably have heard about static equilibrium. Perhaps, you also encountered dynamic equilibrium. What's the difference between the two terms?

When a system is at rest, it's called a static equilibrium. When two or more forces are well-matched, it means dynamic equilibrium.

A scale, for example, with equal weight on both sides, show static equilibrium. Let's say you fill a bathtub with water. Then, you turn the faucet off, which shows static equilibrium.

However, the time you unplug the drain or turn on the faucet, it's simply a dynamic equilibrium.

Another example of equilibrium is the rule of supply and demand. Warren Buffet, the founder of Berkshire Hathaway, bought approximately 11.2 million ounces of silver.

"For the past years, bullion inventories have declined. Last summer, Charlie and I came up with a conclusion that a higher price can play a big role in establishing the equilibrium between the supply and demand," Buffet said.

The only way to restore the market with a good state of equilibrium was to raise the prices. Known as the balancing force to supply, demand can also result in a successful and lasting investment. With the knowledge of supply and demand, you can make a better investment decision. You perhaps are thinking of the producers of an aluminum can and other undifferentiated goods. However, they are a poor investment simply because they can only lead to sufficient returns when the supply is tight. When there's excess capacity in the sector, the price rate will decline, and only the owners are left with poor returns on investment.

The low cost producers are the only winners. As prices decrease, they are the ones who can maintain production. Then, high-cost competitors should cut the production to reduce the supply and moves the sector to equilibrium. When everything is back to normal, the production is no exception. However, the low cost producers are single people who can operate throughout the cycle.

Profit opportunities from equilibrium only take place when the demand exceeds the capacity, which in turn can lead to a positive or negative change in demand and supply. Although this equilibrium is simple, it remains incomplete, but we should consider reflexivity.

"Reflexivity helps shape all participants' thinking, which can develop the reality throughout the process. Although both thinking and reality approach each other, they would never be identical at the end of the day," George Soros writes.

Think with System 2

Daniel Kahneman's best-selling book entitled Thinking, Fast and Slow tackles about the two modes of thought such as the System 1 and System 2. What is the difference between the two terms?

The system 1 is fast, frequent, stereotypic, emotional, and unconscious. It can identify that a specific object is at a greater distance compared to other things, find the source of a sound, read different texts on a billboard, make a good chess move, and understand sentences.

Below are the other things they can perform:

- Display disgust every time they see a terrible image.
- Solve basic addition.
- Drive a vehicle, especially on an empty road.

System 2, on the contrary, is slow, logical, conscious, calculating, infrequent, and effortful. It can direct your interest especially to the clowns and other performers at the circus. It can help dig in your memory to recognize every sound, identify an appropriate behavior during a formal gathering, park into a tight space, identify the validity of a logical reasoning, and more.

Here are the other things that the system 2 can do:

- Brace yourself before the beginning of a sprint.
- Direct your attention to a person at a party.
- Look out for an individual with grey hair.
- Sustain an above-average walking rate.
- Ascertain both the quality and price of an appliance.
- Solve more complex multiplication equation.

So, which is better between System 1 and System 2 for you to see more clearly? Well, think with the latter to make a logical decision making. No matter how difficult a situation you face along the way, System 2 can make you reasonable at all times.

After decades of extensive research and contribution to a range of fields, Daniel Kahneman won the Nobel Memorial Prize in Economic Sciences. He also received the National Academies Communication Award for his work, which helps the public to understand engineering, medicine, behavioral science, and other fields.

As with looking for equilibrium point and ignoring a black swan event, thinking with system 2 takes a long time and practice. Although this mode of thought is slower, it is driven by logic and deliberation. Furthermore, System 2 can drive many of your life choices.

Chapter 9: Learning Organization

As a term, a learning organization is given to a company or business that facilitates the learning of their employees so that the former would continue to grow in the industry. Learning organization exists due to the pressure that small- or big-sized companies face for the past years to remain competitive and productive in the sector. Coined by Peter Senge and his colleagues, learning organization leads to an interconnected and effective way of thinking. Such companies become a community, in which all employees feel committed to help the former realize their goals.

Over the years, the concept is hailed as a panacea for a business success in a diverse and complicated economy. Due to the complexity or uncertainty of the environment, the concept remains increasingly relevant to all parts of the industry. *"The rate at which businesses of all sizes learn may serve as a sustainable and effective source of advantage,"* Senge said.

While the idea seems inspiring, people find it hard to implement and incorporate. It involves a profound change in the employees' mind. The organization's culture and society are no exception. Also, such a change is a long and stressful process. It does not happen in a snap. Aside from ample time, it requires your attention, effort, and other resources.

What is a learning organization in a deeper sense?

- *"Learning organizations are organizations where all professionals expand their capacity to turn their expected results into a reality. It's where new patterns of thinking are fostered, and aspiration is set free,"* Peter Senge added.

- *"Learning organization is an organization with the philosophy for anticipating and responding to both complexity and uncertainty."*

- According to McGill, together with his colleagues, a learning organization is a company that can effectively respond to information by changing their programming.

- A learning organization is a company that can modify its perspectives and behaviors due to their years of experience and wide expertise. While this sounds an obvious statement, most organizations are unable to acknowledge the facts and repeat the same behavior.

These days, the competition is tough while the market is changing and uncertain. That's why any organizations need to survive and grow. Obviously, managers have a lot of responsibilities to perform. Using their skill and sound judgment, they have to make the right decisions when a problem takes place. Effective decision making requires businesses of all sizes to develop and enhance their ability of learning behaviors within a short span of time. This new insight into a startup or big companies is considered a fighting process when facing the pace of change. Throughout this procedure, managers should increase both the awareness and the employee's ability to understand or manage both the environment and the organization itself. In this case, they can make smart decisions, secure the company, and make their objectives happen.

Nowadays, managers guarantee organizational learning. However, they are unable to understand how to make and develop their company a learning organization.

Both groups and individuals learn. This is especially true when there are well-designed systems and conditions. They can share new learning across the company and incorporate it into its existing practices and culture.

People who have a leadership role in a learning organization act as a designer, steward, and teacher to establish a shared vision and challenge existing mental models. They are responsible for learning while the employees are expanding all their capabilities to become more competitive in the coming years.

The basic concept for a learning organization is that only flexible and adaptive companies will excel during emergency situations. In this case, the businesses themselves need to improve employees' dedication and ability to learn at different levels.

With a goal to bring new ideas, the learning organization also aims to debate current issues, introduce effective strategies, and provide timely case studies.

At present, professionals in different fields consider learning organization a process. Over time, the concept of a learning organization as an apolitical end-state will gain acceptance in different parts of the globe.

What's the key factor in building a successful learning organization? Well, it relies on how the companies process their managerial expertise and experience. The ability of a startup or big businesses is not measured by what they know. It's assessed by how they learn instead. Management practices also encourage creativity, empathy, systematic thinking, and a sense of efficacy.

Although every employee can learn, the working environment is not conducive to proactive engagement and holistic reflection. That's not all! Everyone lacks the tools and other guiding ideas to handle daily situations and challenges. Aside from ensuring success in a business operation, the learning organization aims to create and develop a good future for employees and other concerned individuals.

The mastery of basic disciplines makes a learning organization different from the conventional organization. Peter Senge's five disciplines are converging to transform a learning organization into a more innovative company, according to experts. These can include Building a Shared vision, systems thinking, mental models, team learning, and personal mastery.

A Simple Overview of Senge's Five Disciplines

"Approximately one-third of 500 businesses will disappear in 15 years. The lifetime for the largest companies, on the contrary, is around 40 decades," Peter Senge said. This concept enables today's organizations to experience constant growth, perform effectively, and stand out from the competition.

Rather than visualizing a conventional hierarchy, companies can address the challenges when they create a strong and effective learning organization. Senge's five disciplines describe the proper way of managing a business' success or development. They also give everyone an idea of how employees exceed their company's expectations.

5 Disciplines of Senge's Learning Organizations

1. Building a Shared Vision

In every learning organization, those with leadership goals should create and develop the vision together with the employees. Most leaders have personal objectives. However, they don't share it to the lifeblood of any business – employees.

By compromising the company's and employee's goals, it's possible to create a shared vision. With that, turning a business performance into a learning mechanism and changing the relationship will be a reality.

2. Systems Thinking

The learning organizations was developed from systems thinking, a conceptual framework, which enables everyone to study businesses. Whether you evaluate a company or has ample information systems, learning organization uses this system thinking. This Sense's discipline states that every character should be visible in a company, making it a learning organization. But what will happen when these characters are missing? Simply, business falls short of its objectives.

But some experts believe that the characteristics are gradually acquired. In simple terms, they are not developed simultaneously.

Servers as the cornerstone of a learning organization, system thinking integrate employees of a business, making them a body of theory or practice.

Rather than focusing on specific issues, this discipline indicates the process of a whole system. That's why anyone with leadership rules should remember that both action and outcomes are correlated with one another.

Sometimes, managers only focus on specific actions, which in turn can result in overlooking the big picture. But when they understand the correlation, system thinking allows us to see the relationship of change in a specific situation. They will also identify the cause and effect of every problem along the way.

3. Mental Models

Called as ingrained assumptions or generalizations, mental models influence how we take action and understand the things that surround us.

To make the shift to a learning organization fast, it's important to challenge these mental models. In this fast-paced world, individuals are likely to adopt theories. In most cases, businesses have memories that preserve behaviors, values, and norms.

When establishing a learning environment, adopt an open culture to promote trust, and replace any confrontational attitudes. To realize this goal, the mechanisms for identifying and evaluating organizational theories are highly imperative.

The mental models begin when they turn the mirror inward. Simply, we are capable of unearthing internal pictures about the world, which hold them to scrutiny. More than that, it includes the skill to continue any meaningful conversations, balancing advocacy, and inquiry.

If businesses of all sizes develop the ability to work with this discipline, the workforce needs to acquire sets of skills and improve new orientations. But institutional changes and openness in a company can be critical.

4. Team Learning

Individual learning encompasses of team learning, which allows the employees to grow professionally. With access to expertise and knowledge, it can improve the organization's problem solving capacity. A learning organization is packed with structures that encourage team learning with openness, boundary-crossing, and other features. Team learning also requires individuals of different levels to engage in discussion. However, team members need to foster open communication, shared insights, and shared meaning as well. A learning organization has superb knowledge management structures, which can lead to the creation, acquisition, and implementation of the knowledge in the business of all sizes.

A lot of organizations also view team learning as the process of aligning or developing a specific team's capacities to achieve their expected results. Not only can it build on personal mastery, but it can also lead to a shared vision. Unfortunately, these are not enough. All employees should work together to maximize good outcomes and guarantee personal development in the long run.

The concept of team learning begins with a dialogue and the member's capacity to stop assumptions and make genuine thinking.

The idea of team learning among a company's employees supports them to be open-minded to the flow of wider and greater intelligence. Combined with systems thinking, every dialogue can create a suitable and relevant language to deal with any complexity. Instead of being diverted by questions of leadership style, everyone can focus on structural forces and other issues.

5. Personal Mastery

When a person clearly visualizes his goals with a perception of reality, personal mastery takes place. What drives the employees to practice all activities to make their objectives happen? The gap between reality and vision encourages them to go beyond their limitations.

However, this tension depends on how a professional understands an existing reality. Sharing the truth is an important fundamental for this Senge's discipline. But a business' employees could believe they lack the skills to realize their objectives. *"We should spend time to train and bring the potential of our subconscious mind to handle complex problems as effectively as possible, "*Peter Senge said.

Why is a Learning Organization of High Importance?

Rather than relying on ad hoc process to achieve organizational learning thru serendipity, a learning organization encourages and boosts collective learning. While it can maximize successful business results, it can provide other advantages and here are some of them:

- Small- or medium-sized companies can remain competitive and productive in the industry despite the competition. They can also keep a high level of innovation and incorporate new trends into their business.

- They can respond to new and external pressures. They can become flexible and effective, enabling them to provide the best services to various and potential clients.

- A learning organization can enable businesses to link their existing resources to their customers' growing and changing needs.
- It improves the quality of outputs and services at different levels. Despite the difficulty of every stage, products or services will remain responsive and relevant.

- It improves the image of a company and makes it people-oriented over time. From building brand awareness to establishing a good reputation, the possibilities are endless.

- It also increases the pace of change in startups and other businesses. The industry is changing. But it's hard to incorporate that change into a business. With a learning organization, it lessens the complexities, makes the process simple, and guarantee success.

Chapter 10: Become One with Nature

Classic science is more likely to consider nature as something external to regulate and foresee. Scientists try to know the forces of nature and harness them for the gain of humanity. That usage of nature could be positive, which result in different technological innovations that save lives and make living simpler.

The initial phase in joining our body, along with nature, is thinking that we are part of nature. We are not separate from it, but we are a vital part of it all. Our body is composed of all the same energy, elements, and minerals, which creates our planet. The majority of scholars and quantum physicists think that all things in the outer universe are only a mirror of our consciousness as well as our body. For instance, the ratio of water in the Earth mirrors the similar ratio of water within our bodies and more.

It is a fact that people are nature-beings. However, we could still fall out of arrangement along with our natural characters. You see, wellness is in melody with nature. It supports ourselves with the innate understanding, which is within everybody.

For instance, we get tired for a specific time at night that is the natural circadian rhythm of the body that works. No matter if you like to go to sleep at a particular time, it is always up to you. Most of the time, not listening to the cues of your body could be the difference between sickness and health.

One research tells that what everybody feels and knows lessens stress. It's also believed that spending some time in nature is considered anti-inflammatory. The experts discovered that positive emotions felt with nature are connected to low levels of pro-inflammatory cytokines.

If we connect with ourselves, the outdoors, and the signals of our body are the answer in optimal well-being.

Below are some ways so you can connect your body along with nature.

1. Become one with the elements

It could be swimming in the sea or simply camping in the forest. These simple ways could get you into nature. You must understand about the different minerals and crystals as well as their healing abilities. You could also learn the various animals, flowers and plants and every creature of life.

Feel the air and breathe it in a place abundant with trees. You can also climb a mountain or a boulder. Silently listen to the birds. The sweet sounds of nature and the wind in the trees. Perform meditative types of movement like yoga, qi gong, and tai chi in nature.

Start imagining the roots mounting into the earth from your arms and your feet as the twigs of the tree. You can think of what fruits you bare and what it's grounded into. Visualize you're an eagle in the blue sky. Where would you like to go, and how would you feel? Picture yourself if you are one of your favorite animals. Can you feel their vitality inside your form?

2. Listen to what your body tells

Listening to your body is very simple. When you are feeling tired, sleep. If you are starving and craving for food, eat. If you are feeling invigorated, move your body. If you are suffering from pain, listen up, and ask why. You might not know, but it might be that you need some massage. Perhaps you need to stretch more and slowdown from everything you do.

3. Exercise moon and sun gazing

Everyone loves to look up at the moon at night. However, have you ever tried to look for a long time and feel the connection with the brightest thing in the night sky? You understand that the moon is accountable for variations in the seas low and high tides. Are you aware that the moon has a massive impact on your emotional condition too? In fact, a woman's menstrual cycle is directly influenced by the waning and waxing of the moon.

On the other hand, sun gazing is a fascinating exercise, which has been practiced for many centuries. Several individuals even report not wanting any food by just staring into the sun during particular times of the day.

You see, throughout those times, the sun doesn't have any negative impacts on the eyes. It's also believed in boosting eyesight, vitality, and energy as well.

4. Feel the ground

In case you didn't know yet, your skin breathes and absorbs minerals and vitamins from the planet. For instance, when you go barefoot on the ocean, the negative ions from the salts in the sea and sand are known to have healing powers on one's body.

What's more, try digging your feet into the soil, as it's also known to have benefits. You must allow your feet's skin to touch the ground, the grass, and the sea.

5. Gazing the clouds and the stars

Staring upward could be a means to exceed space-time truth. The majority of civilizations stared to the stars to seek power and guidance. Are you familiar with the expression, *"as above, so below?"*

Everyone is composed of stardust. Understanding about the stars could bring us above the mundane and into optimum consciousness. Meanwhile, cloud gazing is, no doubt a fun type of meditation. Stare at the sky above so you can have that pure energy.

6. Transform your mindset

You must understand that nature is not simple on the outside in your environment. You are part of that being too! The identical water, which pours in the sea, also runs over your bloodstream.

The similar minerals and seas you see in nature are the substance from which your body and bones are developed. What's more, the air you breathe is a type of symbiotic connection between trees and humans. That offers the crucial element for one another to flourish and live.

Always remember that your body is built from nature. You present your physical body back to nature at the end of the incarnation. When you perform meditation, and you continuously go outdoors physically, you connect along with your extended body.

As you can see, you can now tap into any part of nature, as it's innately within you. No matter how long you like to stay inside your room, under the fluorescent light or at your desk, you cannot deny the fact that you are nature. Nothing could take that away from you.

Chapter 11: Decision-Making Ability and the Basics

The process of decision-making is selecting among two or more courses of the deed for a particular scenario. Deciding a crucial part of our day-to-day life. A few think of it as an art, some think of it as a proficiency. Your decisions might be expert or individual. Whatever the case, your options will have lasting effects.

In short, the decisions you make have the chance to impact yourself and other people both temporarily and continuously. Thus, you must acquire the necessary skill set, which will enable you to weigh and reflect your choices. You must choose the best decision, which will be most suitable for every scenario.

Laymen and professionals equally have presented a numerous recommendations about how to become a proficient decision-maker. A few support an elementary method, like establishing a mental checklist referred to when a person is confronted with options. A few want to execute a complicated set of processes, which must end in best results.

Determine the Concern or Goal that Needs a Decision

The initial step is to determine the decision which you're experiencing. The issue might be easy enough to talk about with basic language, not needing hours of refection.

You need to bear in mind that decision-making isn't connected to an issue. However, it could take the form of goal setting as well. For example, you might be considering about your future, and you say to yourself, *"Going to university is possibly a great choice if I like to make lots of money in the future."* Here, your goal is obvious, even though this is addressed quite innocently.

One way that similar goal could be explained might be with more urbane redundancy like this one: *"I am challenged with the decision of going to college and delaying employment or seeking a work and participating the workforce as soon as possible."* You see, those are the options, which need higher exploration.

Always remember that no matter how your goal or issue is determined; the essential point is the initial step within your decision-making process. You need to state your problem in an understandable and plain language.

Collect Data and Alternatives Linked with Options

You have now a clear idea in mind of the decision you are experiencing. The next step is to research every possible option you have. This will vary greatly on the seriousness of the problem you are suffering, and the fastness the decision should be made.

In the scenario of life choice about attending college, that's a decision, which will need higher research and thought. Relevant data should be collected before determination. You must always keep in mind that this stage also covers looking asking some advice from people in the field as well as the opinions of your trusted friends and family members. Their experience might offer you with practical and valuable insight, which would progress the process.

Ultimately, a gathering of information will lead to the determination of options for every preference. You must integrate those findings into the step of gathering information.

Decide

After the alternatives have been sightseen comprehensively, and you have already a list of options, what's next? It is time that you choose one of the options which have been created. Choosing the ideal solution isn't as simple as it might look. But the real process of making the decision on an alternative will be easier. That's true, particularly if you have put in the dedication and effort to determine the problem and explore your options. That will enable you to move forward with higher self-confidence.

In the example where a young man is considering the benefits and drawbacks of college attendance, you will find different options. Maybe, he could attend college part-time and work part-time at the same time. Perhaps, he can attend a less costly college, allowing him to free up some money for relocating out of the home. In this case, you will find a wide array of options. Thus, the consequences of decision-making are a bit complicated.

It's also the time where a preference should be designated. It's the part in the decision-making process, which could trigger stress. It needs a leap of trust, a level of instinctive instinct, as well as personal understanding. If the person has used enough effort, it will enable him to choose the perfect decision with much confidence.

It's also suggested that even when a decision has been decided, the personal challenged with the task must take time to think. It would be ideal to allow the subconscious mind to do the entire thinking. In short, you have executed the decision-making process to that point. You have already determined the issue, you have also considered the options accessible, and you've made a rational decision according to the data you gathered.

It's time to have faith in yourself to suppress the decision. Pay attention carefully to your internal voice.

Put your Decision into Action and Assess

It's not typical for individuals to postpone their decision making only because they're uncertain about making life-defining decisions. However, that's part of becoming an adult. Every time you implement that process, you also become more competent and adept in the skill. You become more assured of your own ability to use it for your own gain.

Whatever decision you are challenged with making, you need to act on it later on. You will find an exhilarating sensation, which comes with action. Especially if it's based on the right application of the process of decision-making.

The young man who's trying to make the decision whether or not to attend college has decided that he'll require an advanced education if he likes to participate in the work setting. He has limited funds but doesn't prefer to live at home. Therefore, he decided to enroll in a close community college. He also discovered a full-time employment, and he is relocating into a good apartment close to his school.

The decision maker in the example we presented is happy with his decisions. He is always more content with his capability to manipulate the process of decision-making to his gain. Through the following weeks or months, he will assess the decisions he has made to identify if it's the best option for his case. He will also determine whether the plan should be adjusted in some manner.

The presentation of the decision-making process has improved his skills in the steps, which are needed to steer the choices of life.

Are you currently trying into this study? Do you like to become a more skillful individual, if not expert? When we talk about decision-making, it's relevant to keep in mind the four basic steps of the process.

Make sure that you state the problem first in a plain and clear language. Next, do all your research on every option accessible to handle the issue. Then, you need to make the decision from the alternatives measured. Finally, ratify the decision and assess to make sure that it's a suitable one to reach its specified purpose.

Take note that practice always makes perfect. That's basically significant when we talk about decision-making.

Chapter 12: Deal with Conflict

Every time you are surrounded by people, there will always be a conflict. Opinions always differ, and misunderstandings and miscommunications take place. Individuals have unique urgencies and standards in their lives, and the majority battles change.

All of those establish conflict in everyone's work and life. The issue is not the conflict itself. It is how people deal with it. Fortunately, having efficient conflict management approach could be understood and mastered easily. In this section, allow us to present some tips on how you can efficiently handle interpersonal conflict.

- **Stay away from troublemakers**

   This type of people will only suck you in and drag you all the way down. We encourage that you do not interact in backstabbing or any type of gossip. You must get the facts properly before you shift to conclusions about something you heard through the branches.

   You must be aware of when it is time to walk away from a confrontation. Consider always the main source in the face of upsetting comments or criticisms.

- **Improve your communication skills**

The skill to communicate yourself openly will enable you to tell what is on your mind. It also enables you to request what you need and want, as well as helping you get your point across. You might be familiar with the maxim that a problem well specified is a problem half-resolved.

- **Work to lessen conflict**

You need to take the necessary steps to lessen conflict at work before it takes place. Work at establishing good relationships along with colleagues and coworkers. You must get to know other people as well. You need to become sociable and friendly too.

Keep in mind that everybody has various priorities and needs. They also come from various cultural backgrounds. As opposed to what you normally have heard, familiarity breeds respect.

- **Pick your battles**

You will always find various opinions and ways of doing stuff. Make the decision to which problems you could live and determine which of them need dealing with. You will establish credibility if you know how to bring only the most vital problems. Meanwhile, you will be named a complainer if you make an issue about all thing.

- **Say sorry when suitable**

You need to become mindful of your own part when establishing the conflict. Have you ever done something wrong or not appropriate? Then, it's suitable that you acknowledge and say to others that you are sorry. That's right even when the conflict is not an outcome of your actions. Often, you will have to meet people in the middle to get where you wish to go.

- **Take advantage of a mediator if needed**

Do your efforts haven't worked the way you want it? Then you can invite a neutral third party when the situation is worrying or instable. You can invite a supervisor to serve as an intermediary if it's amenable to everyone concerned.

That person could remain objectively, listen to every party, and simplify resolution and cooperation. You must be firm on your goals. Remember that you are there to fix a conflict and not to reverse an enemy.

- **Discuss it personally**

Let's face it; meeting in person is always intimidating. However, it is often the ideal option to go. You see, direct communication is much efficient than other types, as it enables for an active exchange of data. It also offers you the chance to utilize hand gestures, eye contact, smile, handshake, and other types of body language.

That enables you to perceive vital non-verbal signals from the other side. You need to set aside some time to meet along with the other individual personally at a convenient place and time. Instead of meeting on one of your offices, ensure you meet on a "neutral turf."

Furthermore, writing of a letter, messaging, social media, and email must be prevented. Doing this will prevent talking about sensitive topics, problems, and hurting other's feelings. Take note that it's not direct and impersonal when you use these mediums. You also raise the risk of misunderstanding and miscommunication.

A phone call would be your next option if the in-person meetings were not feasible.

- **Handle it**

The majority of individuals want to stay away from conflict. In fact, some people have actually quit their work instead of trying to fix an interpersonal conflict at their work. But it's never a good answer, as it normally results in feelings of guilt and regret. Aside from that, you will be just quitting your work in a short period if you quit whenever you have a conflict with your work.

Every conflict should be handled appropriately. If you just ignore and stay away from it, it could result in raised stress. It might also present unresolved feelings of resentment, hostility, and anger. You will be healthier and happier in your life if you learn how to handle your conflict efficiently.

You will have a wonderful relationship with other people. You will become a better leader at work, a better member of the team, and a better individual in general. You will earn respect, boost your confidence, and establish your courage.

- **Contemplate it through**

You need to consider talking about the situation with an impartial family member or friend before you address the other person with whom you have a conflict. Doing this could help you clarify needs and problems. Search for advice and feedback whenever you deal with the situation.

However, you must always be watchful not to depend on the opinion of an involved third party. That's because this person might have his or her own goal. You need to plan your strategy very carefully. Device what you wish to say and write it down. Rehearse it if needed.

You can also make a notecard along with your key talking points. That will guide you to feel more in control and stay on your target.

When you're able to lead other people, conflict is sure to arise. In a workgroup, critical conversations on tasks and direction sometimes draw out competing concepts. Various differences rooting from diversity and diverse perspectives also add. The capability to work efficiently through and fix conflict sometimes determines a high performing work group from one, which fails to do.

One of the advantages of conflict resolution is that it improves the assurance among conflict friends. Dealing over the conflict, along with other people, ties the conflict partner as they encounter issues and deal with the trials organized. Moreover, it gets the involved individuals in the conflict discerning in terms of "we" rather than "me." That improves the dedication of both parties to the process of conflict resolution.

Choice quality is enhanced when ideas are vetted. Flaws, which might have been ignored if people prevent talking about the problem are seen, and optimal solutions are created. If you have taken apart in this argument, you are more likely to support the execution of a specific solution, although it might not be your preferred option. That's because you have felt their ideas have been considered and that you've been involved in searching for an answer.

Chapter 13: Unlock People Potential

You and everyone is born in the world with a spotless slate. The similar unlimited potential. However, when you go to other ends, it might look that a few have been gifted with more potential than other people have. The reason behind this is that you go through your journey of life. You establish limitations and boundaries on yourself.

Many of those started way back when you are a young kid. It's when you are still a sponge, who is willing and is craving to absorb information of the world around you and the world beyond you. You depended mostly on your parents, your sibling, and your close family. Later on, you widened to your friend's teachers, and far along with relationships at work.

Throughout those vital development phases, you are imprinted with the values and belief of such individuals. You mostly based the majority of your values and beliefs on such foundations.

Unluckily, as young kids, you are often told, *"You aren't intelligent!" "You won't be worthy at anything you do!" "You are a loser"* and other stuff. When those phrases come from the individuals you trust and respect the most, you then believe it. Once those sorts of beliefs are brought through life, your esteem, self-confidence, and potential reduce.

Therefore, if you're currently on a point on your mission that you believe you could do more, or become more, below are some of the stuff you could to change your thinking:

1. **No excuses**

    You must stick with every change you decide. We understand that change could be difficult, particularly when doing the stuff you have not done before. That denotes establishing new habits, which will be not comfortable on you, part.

    Plan your next day every night. Think of the things you need to be completed and how do you plan to do it. Remember, the least sum of disclosures you have every day is going to stop you from being sidetracked. You also need to get into every day along with a hundred percent attitude.

    We know that change could sometimes be difficult. However, as long as you create a decision to transform, you will be on your way. Prefer to learn. Transform into a much positive internal language. Adopt every challenge throughout the way. Be stimulated by the challenges. If you need some assistance, go for it.

2. Believe you always can

As we stated earlier, most of your beliefs were imprinted when you are still a kid. We acquired them, and you could *'unlearn'* them if you want. From there, new and fresh values could be established. Once you do this, your unconscious mind will work along with them. That will help you establish results, which will be dependable to them.

These days, you will come across different individuals who will judge and criticize you to who you are. They will do what they can just to cut you down, but that's all right. These people do not have similar values and beliefs as you, nor do they perceive the same image as you. Therefore, be focused on your journey without walking on to theirs.

3. Establish an image

You must understand what you truly desire if you like to make some changes. Ask yourself, *"What is my true potential?" "What does it look?" What am I doing in the picture?"* You must let yourself sense the feelings and hear the sounds.

You will have no idea of what you're striving if you do not picture your result. It does not matter what image is suitable today, as it could change in the future. What's important is that you have something to start.

4. Develop your mindset

Some individuals live with a Fixed Mindset. These individuals think that their intellect, potential as well as a character, is outlined and established after they are born. On the other hand, individuals with a Growth Mindset think that their intellect, potential as well as character could be enhanced.

They also think that everyone is born with a clean slate. Each individual in this world could be whatever he or she likes to be. They choose to enhance their life situation by understanding and adopting themselves and by failing.

You must distinguish such two mindsets and make sure you have the latter. It's vital as well that you decide to change it if you think your mindset belongs to the Fixed.

5. Accept who you truly are as a person

You can establish a vision of moving forward by understanding where your life is and approving you are where you always meant to be. Do you feel life indebted you for your past? Then you're just waiting for it to be presented to you. That will take you a very long period.

Indeed, a few events in your life might not have been fair to you. Some of them might have hurt you, and some might have been totally wrong. Nevertheless, if you will hold onto those and emotions are connected to them; that will only keep you where you are today. Learn to accept where you are now and decide to change.

Few individuals think that we are here in the world for a reason, a particular purpose. Some think they are here only because they are, without a given goal. No matter where you fit on that scale is just fine. Irrespective of where that is, you must aim to be the best version of you that you could possibly be. That's what truly means of living to your real potential.

Use these strategies above to unlock your potential and help others to unlock their potential as well. As leaders, you create an impact each day on the people around you. It is your decision, whether it is a good one or not. Assisting other people to unlock their own potential is the best gift you can offer them. Take the time to assist other people to grow and learn. You will be surprised at what could take place once you release their potential. Who knows, it might just beginning a chain reaction of development.

Chapter 14: How Avoidance Breeds Success

Each of us has our own desires, aims, and drives in lives that we wish to accomplish. However, the majority of individuals do not consider the *"strings attached"* to the difficult journey they are beginning. For that reason, we sometimes experience lots of emotional and mental failure, resulting in a downward shift in your action, confidence, and willpower.

These might come as a huge surprise to you. After all, every one of us has been refined to study very hard since we were children, top every exam and receive that diploma. All of those to accomplish the bet goal to become successful.

Avoid direct goals

That typically agreed guidance is famous when you feel dazed with your life. This could be either at work or at home. That takes place when trials and stuff you like are the decision of others. It might be your wife or husband, your manager, and in other cases, your kid.

Everything exerts some sort of control over you and your life. What is the reason why you must avoid direct goals?

The concern with the assistance of concentrating on what you could govern is that it could result as if not anything is under your control. Especially when the things you cannot control are the most vital in your life. Breaking down the emotional fences of your loved ones, having time for yourself, getting a raise – have an impact on what you cannot control.

It is better if you achieve indirect goals rather than setting direct goals. An indirect goal is when your decisions and direct behaviors impact the activities as well as the decision making of others. The effect of anything indirect is not measurable.

For instance, visualize a dartboard. Your aim is to hit the goal. Well, that's a good example of a direct goal. You perform a direct action, which is tossing the dart. You could also notice the outcome of that direct action – the location of the dart when it hits. You amend your toss and try another. You can perform that as long as required to accomplish the direct goal.

Then, turn the lights off now. It is total black. How can you hit the goal? Try to throw your dart. You could probably hear where your dart lands, but you cannot see how close you are to the target. It is also not possible to make some adjustments. All you could do is toss where you believe the bullseye might be and have some faith that you hit the mark. That's how it feels overlooking the things you do not have control. Sounds difficult, right? That's where indirect goals enter.

Visualize that you can to turn on a light after every toss. You could check where your previous dart landed. You could then arrange the following throw before the light turns off once more. It is still much difficult to hit the board if the light is turned on. However, that's much better than not having any lights to help you. That kind of method is known as *"shining a light"* on the outcomes. It rearranges according to what you could tell. Retrying is a thought of accomplishing things you like even if you do not have control over it.

It will take you some patience and time to accomplish an indirect goal. But it will surely pay off in the long run.

Avoid thinking like an expert

Nowadays, it appears as if everybody is an expert at everything. From your co-worker to your old classmate, everybody you know is an expert at anything they recently obtained.

For instance, a "mom bod" drops 30 pounds in just 2 months and posts her results on Facebook, Instagram, and other platforms and – viola! – we have another health expert accommodating applications for training customers.

Another example would be, a businessperson makes some great decisions. Then suddenly, he becomes a "business coach" to keen viewers, prepared to make it huge. You see, everybody becomes an expert nowadays. Nevertheless, they are not really.

Take note that expertise does not denote you know more than your friends about a particular subject. It denotes you are informed more than the majority of people about a particular subject. It denotes you have understood your arena and that you have spent long hours of learning your skills before you start informing someone on how to do it. That also means that you have performed all the work.

You need to bear in mind that it does not mean you cannot share your work with other people. What it truly means is that you cannot exercise it in a public way that is both humble and honest, helping other people as you go. It only denotes you should not throw around words such as *"expert."*

We are not trying to shock you from assisting anyone with your own experience and sharing what you have already obtained from life. We only need to be cautious about how you position yourself. Perhaps, you must stop calling yourself and thinking like an expert. Instead, start thinking like you're a student.

The world does not need more and more experts. What we truly need are learners. The world requires a group of individuals who is happy to learn their own expertise for 10 years before they begin a blog teaching others how to perform it. The world requires students, and not endless numbers of teachers. The world requires more doers and fewer talkers.

You must be careful right there. An individual isn't an expert only because they think and say they are. Take note that *expert* is only a label you gain only when other individuals notice you are doing something the same thing over again; that's the time they'll start to cry it out on your behalf.

Only because you did something on one occasion does not make you the expert on that topic. It only denotes you lived through an experience that is effective but does not make you become an expert.

Avoid to-do Lists

No matter if you are a keen supporter of a to-do list or you are a hating list-maker, the majority of us keep one. However, your to-do lists somewhat overwhelm and frustrate.

You see, you always overload your list. Social psychologists tell that one individual has approximately 150 various tasks at a time. A CEO's to-do list for one day could take more than one week to complete. Another research claims how comprehensive planning works if you have one huge to-do task. Simply put, the longer the list of your goals and tasks, the less powerful a tool of this to-do list becomes.

You need to bear in mind that overstuffing your list triggers a tenacious thrum of anxiety in your head. That will only obstruct you from handling every working task. It is also found out that stress that comes from having many contradictory goals results in your productivity, mental and physical health to suffer.

Your to-do list helps your recall different things you need to deal within a day or a week. However, it is also a nagging tool, which could trigger risky and disarming stress to your body.

While a to-do list is helpful for organization of your task, they are not the best tool for your productivity issues. As an alternative, you can convert them to *done list*. Did you know that jotting down what you achieve increases the insight and encouragement, which balances out the shortcomings and issues of your to-do list?

The boost you receive from having a visible track record drives you to handle what is next while failing to determine how much you do makes it simple to lose perspective. Your brainpower and time are too important to spend on thinking about everything you must be doing. As an alternative, seek balance and wisdom from recognizing the authenticity of your achievements.

Avoid the path of least resistance

The journey of least resistance is a truth of nature. The rivers move around the mountain instead of flowing through it. The electricity flows through the simplest route. Unluckily, our human nature is the same.

Human beings are more likely to do what is the simplest. Occasionally, we ignore what is best. For instance, it is much simpler to lose our temper with our partner than to control it.

It is much simpler to sit in front of the television rather than spending our time with our children. It is much simpler to read a magazine instead of reading the Bible.

Succeeding the path of least resistant could turn out to be a habit, helping guide our lives. Most of the time, we make choices according to what is least hurting, most enjoyable, and simplest.

Bear this in mind: the secret to success depends on the very thing you are avoiding. Such things appear to break you down and shy your spirit. Search for discomfort. You must become unhurried about doing other stuff, which pushes your limits remarkably.

Difficulty helps you grow as a person. If you are seeking for long-term success, you must stop preventing what is hard and start embracing it. You are not comfortable if you are driving yourself to advance.

Every time you are challenged, you are obliged to be more than you are. That simply denotes establishing new viewpoints, obtaining new abilities, and pushing boundaries. In short, you need to widen your comprehension to surpass the challenges you are experiencing. Learning to become at ease with uneasiness is one of the vital abilities you could have to live a satisfying life. You could master nearly anything once you learn that skill.

One thing you could do is to break the chain of simple routines. Start reading a book you typically disregard. Search and listen to music from those inexperienced composers. You can also participate in workshops or events you have been disregarding. Start that complicated discussion with your officemate at work.

You must not hang out along with the similar individuals who share the same perspective, beliefs, and tastes just like you do. Start getting to know somebody who has a different background. Stepping up when it is painful or annoying establishes your character. Learn how to make time on what really matters to you. Always avoid the path of least resistance.

Chapter 15: The Murphy Law

Are you the kind of individual who thinks that anything which could go wrong, will go wrong when you least anticipate it, at the worst possible time? If yes, you are existing under the power of *Murphy's Law*.

The majority of individuals will understand this law as a negative perception of life. They could not be far from reality. Remember that Murphy's Law is designed under the robust values of forward-thinking and organizing efficient possibility plans, which will help defend against potential hindrances. It lessens the negative effect of the obstructions, which lay before you.

This law catches your imagination. Murphy's Law, as well as its offshoots, has been gathered in web sites and books. Various brands are also named after this law, and it's a sought-after name for many taverns and Irish pubs all across the globe.

However, you must understand that Murphy's Law is a new idea, which dates back in the mid of the previous century. The magician Adam Hull Shirk wrote in his essay that in a particular magic act, 9 out of ten things could go wrong. Before that, it was referred to as the *Sod's Law,* telling that any unfortunate thing could take place to poor sod will. Murphy's Law is still called *Sod's Law* in the country of England.

Origins of the Murphy's Law

Have you heard of Edward J. Murphy? Unbelievably, he was a real individual. He was a major in the United State Air Force in the 1940s who specializes in development engineering. Murphy's work was involved mainly in testing experimental designs, and he was challenged with stuff that did not go to plan. Scholars vary on what words were utilized originally when the phrase *Murphy's Law* was initially invented. Still, the meaning is crystal clear.

Murphy and his crew were breaking new ground. They were not able to depend on the type of proven methods employed efficiently elsewhere in the military to guarantee zero defects. Therefore, they need to rely on their own resourcefulness to get things done.

In 1949, officers were doing project MX981 tests to know how many Gs *(the force of gravity)* a human could endure. They believed that their conclusions could be used to design future airplanes.

The team then utilizes a rocket known as the *Gee Whiz*. That will enable them to fuel the fire of the airplane smash. The sled traveled over two hundred miles every hour down. It comes to a sudden halt in less than a second. The only concern is that the team should have an individual who will experience how much force a person could endure.

That's where Colonel John Paul Stapp comes in. Stapp was a career physician for the Air Force who steps up to try the rocket sled. Throughout various months, Stapp took a ride after punishing journey. He was imperiled to destroyed vessels in the eyes, concussions, wrecked bones, just for the sake of science.

Murphy also participated in one of the tests. He has a set of sensors, which could be used to the harness. Such sensors can calculate the exact quantity of G-force applied once the rocket sled break.

The initial trial after Murphy hanged up his sensors to the harness generated no reading. That's because every sensor had been connected inappropriately. For every sensor, there are two different ways of linking them. He found out that every sensor was installed incorrectly.

After Murphy found out the error, he complained something about the operator who was accused of the mishap. Murphy said that if there are two different ways to perform something, and one of such were led in disaster; the person would do it that way.

Murphy immediately goes back to Wright Airfield where he was posted after that incident. However, Stapp determined the universality of what Murphy had stated. In a press conference, Stapp said that the good safety record of the rocket sled team has been because of the attentiveness of Murphy's Law. He expressed to the media that what is meant is *"whatever could go wrong, will go wrong."*

Universal Truths

Even though this law catches the world-weary, negative view of the world, it does not stand alone. Sharp spectators have now come up with a few of their laws later its fame after the rocket sled trials at Edwards Air Force Base.

A few have become sought-after in their right. One example of this is the *Peter Principle*, telling that every individual will be supported by his or her degree of ineffectiveness. You will find hundreds of rules, observations, and principles, which have been made after Murphy's Law. A few of them are strange, some are funny, and some are wise.

The Appeal and the Fatalism of Murphy's Law

What makes Murphy's Law a universal principle? In spite of everything, you have a 50% chance of getting things right when approaching an electrical socket along with a 2-divided plug engineered to fit one way only. You also have a 50% chance of getting things wrong, as well. Maybe, the perfect clarification to this is the underlying sense of fatalism.

In case you didn't know yet, fatalism is the concept telling everyone is defenseless to the urges of fate. That type of perspective tells that the things, which occur to every person, are inevitable. It is the concept that there is universal law at work, which takes a delight at playing with you.

However, fatalism opposes another principle – free will. That is the concept that human beings acquire the free will and that every choice, together with the effects that come with those options is your own.

Probably, our link to this law is the outcome of the collision among fatalism and free will. Meanwhile, Murphy's Law shows us our own irrefutable foolishness. If allowed to do something not right, we will do so around half of the time. However, that depends on our own options. This law also showcases how they are lacking in control.

Murphy's Law does not ascertain anything. It does not even discuss anything. It only tells a saying: *things will go wrong.* Nonetheless, we fail to recall that there are other powers at work when you contemplate this law. Rudyard Kipling said that how many instances you drop a piece of bread, it will always land on the ground butter-side down. Recognized as the author of *The Jungle Book,* Kipling was made an observation, which many people can always relate to – life is complicated, almost to a ridiculous level.

Talking about the buttered piece of bread, you must remember the reality that one side is always heavier than the other. That denotes that on its way to the earth, the weighty part will flip to the surface because of gravity. However, it won't flip through around back to the top for a similar reason. Consequently, it's weightier than the part without the butter. That makes Kipling correct. A slice of buttered bread will land butter-side down.

Always take note that Murphy's Law is all about life. It talks about the significance of forward-thinking and changing your point of view about the negative scenarios life throws you away repeatedly.

From another view, Murphy's Law refers to recognizing the opportunities. The seeds inside each problem must grow into affirmative results whenever you take a new test. Ultimately, Murphy's Law is all about YOU. This tackles how you approach life and converting your "lemons" into a fresh bottle of lemonade. It will always be up to you if you can work it or not.

Chapter 16
Occam's Razor

The simplest explanation is normally the correct one. You have probably heard this statement before. Detectives utilize it to assume who is the possible suspect in a murder case. Also, doctors utilize it to identify the illness behind a collection of symptoms.

That line of reason is known as the *Occam's razor*. It is utilized in a broad spectrum of ways around the globe as a way to divide a situation or a concern and to remove unnecessary elements. However, what we refer as the razor is a bit different from what its author penned.

You will find two different parts, which are known the basis of Occam's razor:

1. **The Principle of Parsimony** – It's impractical to do along with more what's finished with less.
2. **The Principle of Plurality** – It must not be postulated without necessity.

They symbolize the foundation of the study of humankind into the universe. It also represents the way you perceive your surroundings. There is no telling which type of world you would reside in now without Occam's razor.

You can consider basic systems found in nature, such as plants and viruses and their capability to perform complicated task like photosynthesis and infection. People put importance to such basic models. When we talk about fabricated structures, people are more likely to source structures on what they previously know. All of that points to the philosophies of parsimony and plurality.

One crucial aspect this law shows is the subjectivity of how you perceive the world. Indeed, the sky is blue. You are aware by that through starting at it. Nonetheless, what shadow of blue is it?

The Origin of Occam's Razor

You might be thinking that Occam is the name of a person. It's not. Occam is a town located in England where William of Occam was born. He lived in the middle of 1285 to 1349, through the medieval period. It's the era where surnames were not typical, and citizens were recognized by their place of origin.

William lived as a Franciscan monk and a philosopher. He was a pious person who took his vow of poverty. That means he lived only what's needed. The foundation of the Occam's razor was a well-established line of medieval ideas by the time of

William. He obtained the essence of the law and packed it in a manner, which can be easily comprehended. He was able to encapsulate a world of medieval logic through making a couple of easy sentences. He guarantees its safe way into the modern period.

How Does Occam's Razor Work?

You are already aware that Occam's razor is the principle of simplicity or parsimony following the basic theory tends to be real. Occam didn't formulate this principle. It is invented by Aristotle, Aquinas and other great philosophers Occam read. Even though Occam didn't make a debate for the validity of the principle, he was able to utilize it in different ways. That's the main reason why it's connected with him.

For a few, the principle of simplicity tells the world is simple. For instance, Aquinas debates that nature doesn't use two mechanisms where one serves. That understanding is also proposed by its most famous construction: *entities must not be multiplied beyond necessity.*

However, that's a problematic assertion. Today, you know that nature is terminated in both function and form. Even though medieval thinkers were hugely oblivious of evolutionary biology, they support the occurrence of a supreme God. In any case, Occam never makes that kind of supposition, and he doesn't utilize famous construction of the belief.

For him, the law of simplicity obstructs the development of hypotheses, not certain individuals. Occam thinks that theories aren't intended to perform things such as predicting and explaining. Those things could be obtained more efficiently with fewer expectations.

For a few, it might be a common sense. Presume your vehicle stops working and your fuel gauge tells an empty gas tank. It would be funny to assume both that you're out of gas and oil. You just need one hypothesis to explain what has taken place.

Others would object that the law of simplicity can't assure the truth. Even though the razor looks like a common sense, when utilized in science, it could strong and amazing impacts.

Who Utilizes Occam's Razor?

Scientists are the people who utilize Occam's razor the most. Scientist utilizes the law to get from one pint to another in a specific data set to make their way through huge equations.

Some skeptics also utilize the principle as a vital device and as evidence. In case you didn't know yet, skeptics are individuals who are more likely to believe what they could sense. That makes them foils to individuals who have faith in religious beliefs and conspiracy theories.

However, a real skeptic will explain to you that he only utilizes the principle as a tool for consideration various justifications. Skeptics who value the healthy examination of the universe utilize Occam's razor to have the easiest clarification. Nonetheless, they fall short of utilizing it to discount other, more complicated reasons.

But some scientists and skeptics wield the razor similar to a broadsword. To those individuals, it verifies one theory and contradicts to others. You will find two different issues when you are utilizing Occam's razor as a device to disprove or prove an explanation. First, it can identify whether or not something is subjective. It means it depends on the person to interpret its simplicity. Second, there is no proof, which backs the notion that simplicity is equivalent to truth.

It's essential to bear in mind that the concept credited to Aristotle says that perfection is seen in simplicity is a fabricated concept. It is not supported by physics, chemistry, or math. Nevertheless, it is taken by other people as truthful.

You will find a few creationists who will claim that Occam's razor shows their ideology is right. Consequently, its easy explanation to tell that God created everything in the universe. That's far better than telling it was formed by a Big Bang that was followed by different interconnected accidents.

Another example is the evolutionist. That clarification that God is present, but we have no proof that he truly does. That's the same case for atheists who do not believe in God. These people utilize Occam's razor together with the concept of

Aristotle of simplicity corresponding perfection to claim there's no God.

The only issue with such arguments is that what establishes simplicity is subjective. Aside from that, you can't prove that the universe could be any basic.

At this point, you must have enough idea of how Occam's razor is utilized to improve one idea over the other.

Chapter 17: Hanlon's Razor

Have you ever sensed that the universe is all against you? If so, we want you to know that you aren't alone. Everyone has a tendency to think that when something goes wrong, the fault lies in some conspiracy against you.

For instance, your officemate fails to present you a report on time. They ought to be attempting to ruin your job and beat you to a promotion. Your kid falls and ruins a costly plate. They ought to be attempting to annoy you and waste your precious time.

However, the truth is that such explanations you likely to jump are infrequently true. Perhaps you officemate thought today was Thursday, not Friday. Perhaps your kid has sticky hands from playing. You see, that's where Hanlon's razor enters.

What is Hanlon's Razor?

Hanlon's Razor is a very practical mental model. Similar to Occam's razor, it's a vital tool for quick, intelligent cognition and decision-making.

Using Hanlon's razor enables us to establish relationships better. It also enables you to become less judgmental, and it enhances your nationality. It allows you to offer individuals the gain of the doubt and have more empathy. That way, the importance of Hanlon's razor is pronounced in business and relationships matter.

It's widely known that most people spend most of the day communicating with other people. They also make choices according to those. You lead complicated lives wherein things are continuously going wrong *(as what Murphy's law tells)*. When that takes place, a typical feedback is to a fault to the closest person and thinks they have malevolent intent.

Human beings are fast to accuse politicians, companies, their managers, employees, etc. trying to derail them. You overlook how many times you have jostled someone in the street or overlooked to meet your friend on time. As an alternative, the culprit becomes the source of intense annoyance.

To think intent in such a scenario tends to worsen the issue. None of you could ever determine what somebody else wanted to take place. The most intelligent person makes numerous mistakes. Negligence or inability is far likely to be the source than cruelty.

When a scenario causes you to become exasperated o irritated, it could be appreciated to consider when such emotions are acceptable. Sometimes, the ideal way to react to other individuals causing you some problem is by informing them and not to contempt them. With that, you can prevent a repetition of the same scenario.

The Origins of Hanlon's Razor

The words *Hanlon's razor* was invented, Robert J. Hanlon. However, it has been voiced by various individuals throughout history since 1774.

The Advantages of Employing Hanlon's razor

You might find that Hanlon's razor might be advantageous for two different reasons:

1. **It is recommended for you to begin thinking for another reason than malice for negative situations**

   Generally, considering malice as a source of a negative situation will only cause you to feel more stress and anger than thinking of other reasons. Thus, you could benefit from not thinking the worst from the beginning. That's true, especially when it comes to your emotional productivity and emotional wellbeing.

2. **Hanlon's razor could help you see the most logical explanation for different events**

   It is more likely that individuals will do something that is out of their lack of mindfulness than out of a planned desire to cause any danger.

Employing Hanlon's razor could help you evaluate faster the scenarios that you're currently in. It could help you handle those cases in a much better way.

From a philosophical point of view, using this principle could be perceived as *"doing the right thing."* That's because it shares the principle of charity. It represents the concept that you must begin by thinking about the best possible understanding of other people's actions and speeches.

Using that standpoint is also advantageous for non-philosophical motives. Offering individuals the gain of the doubt at first could help you interact with productively. That also makes them cooperate with you more in the end. That's vital in relationships, both professional and personal. This is where thinking that the other individual did something that had undesirable result out of hatred could be harmful if you end up being mistaken.

Hanlon's razor enables you to be ready to take the necessary action that you otherwise would not. For instance, think of a situation where somebody is doing something, which troubles you so much. That could be a scenario where your next-door neighbor is making too much noise. Unconsciously, you might begin to think that they're conscious of what they're doing is troubling you but they do not care. That is the type of mindset, which causes you to think that you must not care to ask them to stop.

Nonetheless, using Hanlon's razor could help you think they're doing it not because they do not put their attention about troubling you. They are not just not aware that what they are doing is troubling you. That could support you to take some good action. For instance, you might ask them to stop that might not have done otherwise.

Employing Hanlon's razor provides different advantages. That includes assisting you to feel less worried. It also helps you interact better with other people. Later on, you will notice how you could use Hanlon's razor to gain from it.

How to Use Hanlon's razor

Hanlon's razor could be used whenever you have time to seek a reason for why somebody has done something, which ended up having negative effects. You will notice particular guidelines, which will help you use Hanlon's razor efficiently. It could be by extending its scope, by understanding how to evaluate the scenario or by accounting for the egocentric bias.

Exemptions to Hanlon's razor

Hanlon's razor is considered a criterion. However, it must be perceived as a guiding principle instead of an absolute truth. You will find some cases where a negative result must be credited to malice instead of obliviousness and foolishness.

That denotes, although you must aim to offer individuals the gain of the doubt where possible, using Hanlon's razor should not cause you to be not prepared and immature. Therefore, every time you are planning to use Hanlon's razor, you must consider the following aspects:

- **What are the costs linked with *improperly* assuming reasons aside from malice?**

  The pricier it would be for you to think wrongly that somebody acted for a reason aside from malice, the more careful you must be when using this principle.

- **What are the possible costs connected with improperly supposing malice?**

  The pricier it would be for you to assume malice improperly, the more inclined you must be to think that whatever occurred had taken place because of a motive aside from malice.

- **How likely it is that an action took place because of reasons aside from malice?**

  The more probable it is that what occurred did not happen because of malice, the more inclined you must be to presenting the other individual the gain of the doubt. Every time you evaluate that probability, you could consider the past actions of the individual. You can also consider their skills, their general personality, and what they stand to gain from acting malevolently.

You will also find other cases where you might prefer not to employ Hanlon's razor. That's because the probability of the other individual acting malevolently is high. Maybe there's a high price to improperly thinking that their actions didn't happen because of malice.

On those situations, it could be advantageous to begin by thinking malice. Then take a different explanation after you have enough proof telling otherwise.

Always remember that those scenarios could be designated using the idea of *"guilty until proven innocent."* That's the opposite of the idea presented by Hanlon's razor, describing *"innocent until proven guilty."*

Always remember that it could be advantageous to utilize a hybrid strategy. For instance, that could involve thinking non-malicious clarification for other's action and getting ready to act when the hateful explanation becomes true.

Chapter 18: Pareto Principle

The Pareto principle is the adage wherein 80 percent of the results are driven from 20 percent of causes. For instance, whenever you are watching movies. It could mean that 20 percent of the movies, which are being presented, in theaters is accountable for 80 percent of ticket sales.

The 'results' and 'causes' that the principle talks about are varied in nature. It depends on the situation at hand. Another example, 'results' could talk about anything from consumer complaints, financial revenue to acquisition knowledge. However, the 'causes' could mean anything from time spent working, to the features of the software and financial investment.

The Pareto principle has been used in different scenarios. In fact, it has predictive value when we talk about individuals and big groups. Because it's simple to implement and very efficient, it can be useful to know how it works.

A Few Samples of the Pareto Principle

One of the most sought-after examples of this principle is connected to Vilfredo Pareto. He was an economist in Italy, which this principle is coined. Vilfredo noticed that 80 percent of the prosperity in his country is acquired by 20 percent of the population.

You will also find other scenarios where the Pareto principle could be applied. Some of these are the following:

1. A research on software engineering discovered that at least 20 percent of the modules cause 80 percent of its operational errors.

2. A research that assessed flow patterns in libraries discovered that at least 20 percent of the books in the library account for 80 percent of its flow.

3. A research that assessed shopping trends at convenient stores discovered that at least 20 percent of the consumers account for 80 percent of the sales of the store.

The Scientific Foundation for the Pareto Principle

You need to bear in mind that the Pareto principle is sourced on the idea of *power laws*. In short, a power law is a kind of functional connection concerning two quantities. A linear transformation in one quantity results to exponential transformation in the other quantity. That means one quantity differs in proportion along with the power of the other.

The Pareto principle recommends that in most scenarios, you could anticipate noticing a Pareto distribution. That's a particular kind of power-law distribution having a negative exponent. That denotes one quantity grows, the other quantity lowers as a power of initial quantity.

For instance, a distribution of Pareto could take place in the connection between several earners and income level. When you raise the income level by three, you can get nine times fewer people to gain that much.

As a particular outcome level raises, the ration of causes accountable for it reduces. That principle applies to a different real-world variable.

Caution about 20/80 Distributions

You might be aware already that the Pareto principle talks about a particular kind of Pareto distribution. The 80 percent of results come from 20 percent of the causes. Nonetheless, the distribution is not limited to an 80-20 division. Often, you will find a variability about the strict distributions that are seen.

For instance, the distribution may include an 85-15 split, 75-25 split, and so much more. For that reason, the specific distribution won't matter anymore. That's true, particularly when you use the Pareto principle. You need to bear in mind that a small quantity of the causes will be accountable for a big part of the results.

How to Use the Pareto Principle

The objective of this law is to help you focus your efforts effectively. It enables you to concentrate on the small number of causes accountable for a big amount of outcomes. That denotes you must concentrate on the 20 percent of the work, leading to 80 percent of the positive results.

An example of this would be the following:

- Are you designing a software product? You must concentrate on the 20 percent of the features, which are vital to the 80 percent of the users.

- Are you studying for your test? You must concentrate on the 20 percent of the material that accounts for 80 percent of the questions.

- Are you operating a commercial business? You must concentrate on working along with the 20 percent of the consumers who produce 80 percent of your revenue.

What's more, it also denotes you must seek a way on how you can deal with it or remove the 20 percent problems accountable for eighty percent of your negative results. A good example of this would be the following:

- Prevent the 20 percent of the physical exercises that cause 80 percent of the accidents.

- Resolve the 20 percent of the bugs that result in 80 percent of the reports.

- Stay away from working the 20 percent of the customers who generate 80 percent of the criticisms.

Always take note that there could be an overlap between the causes, which result in the positive results and the ones, which result in the negative results. Now, what can you do when this takes place? What will you do when 20 percent of the material you need to study will account for 80 percent of the questionnaires on the test? You must take time to comprehend the material even when that causes eighty percent of your problems.

Nevertheless, you will find some cases where the optimal course of action is not that obvious. For instance, when 20 percent of the consumers produce 80 percent of your income, but also 80 percent of the criticisms. When this takes place, you need to take into account your priorities before you decide the best action.

Guidelines When Using the Pareto Principle

In this section, we will provide you some tips you need to bear in mind when using the Pareto principle:

1. **The Pareto principle is not all about the 80-20 distribution.**

   Even though the principle refers to the 80-20 distribution, you might also encounter different types of distributions. It could be 70-30 or 90-10. Seeking for scenarios where a trivial quantity of causes is accountable for a big ratio of results is important. That's the best thing to do instead of seeking a particular proportion between results and causes.

2. **The Pareto principle does not apply in all scenarios.**

You won't find assurance that it will also apply in the circumstance you're dealing with today, even though most usual scenarios present a Pareto distribution. Further, you will find other cases where another distribution might be more valuable.

3. **There tends to be substantial variation even with the top 20 percent and the bottom 80 percent.**

You might notice a huge variation even with people who belong to every group. When your sample is big enough, you might notice that the top 20 percent and bottom 80 percent bottom could be divided using an 80-20 distribution.

For instance, 20 percent of earners within the population. You will find a massive variation amid the upper few individuals who gain the most, and the rest of the crowd.

Are you dealing with a continuing process? Then it's vital that you re-assess your situation every now and then. You could amend after based on the Pareto principle every time. That's because the distribution between the applicable results and causes might change in the long run.

Ultimately, when you apply the Pareto principle, you must ensure to employ common sense. Always consider the further factors, which might be vital beyond the cause-result link. For instance, you are trying to launch a software service. However, you are trying to choose which bugs to resolve according to the number of users who reported them. It's more likely that you like to fix a bug, which could cause crucial security problems, even when one user only noticed it.

Chapter 19: Sturgeon's Law

"90% of all things are crap." That saying is what Sturgeon's law represents. It indicates the belief that most work that is generated in any field is poor quality. For instance, books, the law tells that ninety percent of the books, which come out yearly are comparatively poor.

That idea is an advantageous criterion. Bearing this in mind could help enhance how a person evaluates and use information. It also helps in the way in which a person chooses which tasks to work on.

The Origins of the Sturgeon's Law

Did you know that Sturgeon's Law was initially referred to as the *Sturgeon's revelation?* It was proposed in 1950 by the American author Theodore Sturgeon as part of his cover of the value of science fiction books being printed.

The law was initially mentioned around 1951 in New York University. Later on, it was popularized at the World-Con Science-fiction convention in 1953.

The goal of this law is to point out that even most science fiction writing is poor, that should not be employed to attack science fiction as a genre. That's because most products and works in any type of sectors are poor as well.

For that reason, Sturgeon announced that science-fiction writing is not different from other types of writing. It's true irrespective of the reality that critics condemned it more severely.

Real-Life Examples of the Sturgeon's Law

You will find different instances of this law in different fields. Some of these are the following:

- Most new products launched today are of poor quality. That denotes they are not worth buying.
- Most new television shows today are of poor quality. They are not worth viewing.
- Most new books launched in the bookstores today are poor quality. That means they aren't worth reading anymore.

Indeed, Sturgeon's law thinks that ninety percent of all things are crap. It is hard to enumerate the exact number of works that are of poor quality. In the majority of cases, it's hard to identify what contributes to poor quality and what does not.

That kind of problem is predominant in situations where the supposed quality of a specific work varies on the standpoint of the person evaluating it. For instance, there are some books, which some individuals will consider as excellent while some will consider they are awful. That's because the last group is composed of individuals who are not attracted to the subject the books cover.

That's vital to bear in mind considering the applications of the Sturgeon's law. In most cases, the classification of what's good and what's not is random. It will still vary on the personal preference of the person.

How Can You Use the Sturgeon's Law?

Below are some guidelines you can follow when you decided to apply Sturgeon's law:

- **As a Creator**

  It could be advantageous to apply this law if you are somebody who makes products or content. The principle could guide you determine what type of things to concentrate on within your work.

  You can start by evaluating the existing market. Notice how your work ranks compared to current products. Identify whether or not what you're making is value your time. Mostly, unless you could design work, which is in the top ten percent, there's no point to reproducing it. You will only be backing to the noise. You can simply add to the lower ninety percent of works, which the majority of individuals disregard.

One way you could gain as a creator is that it a small minority of the work that you generate will have to huge effect. But that's alright. Knowing the Sturgeon's law could be advantageous whenever you are learning; helping you set your own realistic goals.

As a creator, you should concentrate on making something, which is unique, given that the products available today are of poor quality. Stop producing something, which contributes to the noise. Concentrate on showing only your greatest work unless you are creating something as part of your learning skill.

- **As a critic**

The principle could be advantageous if you are playing the role of a critic. That's because it could help you think not to waste your time disapproving defective things. After all, those things must not be taken seriously.

Using Sturgeon's law as a critic could be relevant when evaluating things fairly. That's because a big amount of the works given in a field tend to be low quality irrespective of what the field is. Therefore, you must not judge a field because it has subpar works. You must not concentrate on the weaker aspects of something every time you are condemning it.

Based on Sturgeon's law, it could be seen as an extension of the principle of charity. That simply entails that you must concentrate on the stronger features of a claim when condemning it.

You see, it might be simple to concentrate on the inferior features of something when condemning it. However, it will only be a waste of time, leading unlikely to a productive conversation. Thus, you must try to concentrate on stronger elements of whatever it is you're condemning instead of its weaker aspects.

- **As a consumer**

Sturgeon's law is also advantageous for a consumer. It helps you become a more practical person regarding how you use your money, effort, and time. That's true, especially when buying items or consuming information.

One way you can use Sturgeon's law as a consumer is to think of your decision about which product to purchase or which content to consume as a *zero-sum game*. That is where the resources you give to something of inferior quality could instead be devoted to something more valuable.

That denotes each time you waste loading your mind with poor information is a time you could spend on something worthy. Poor and subpar information will only take up significant mental space in the end. That could even lead to transferring high quality material.

You will see different methods that you utilize in an attempt to prevent the low quality of ninety percent of the material out there. For instance, you must check the reviews first before you purchase a book. That will help you decide if it fits your interest and it helps you to know if people trust it's worth reading.

The majority of what is out there is of low quality, whether when it comes to apps, articles, movies, books, and so much more. Do not waste your money and time on those low-quality items. As an alternative, understand how to determine the high-quality stuff, and concentrate on them.

Basic Guidelines

Sturgeon's law must be used along with common sense. Acknowledge the fact that Sturgeon is a practical rule of thumb. It must be valued as such instead of absolute truth.

Often, the ratio of works that's worth of your time might be ten percent. However, sometimes that will end up being the same but different figures, like twenty percent or five percent. Concentrate on the underlying idea behind it rather than trying to quantify the law with exact metrics.

The best works in a particular sector are not randomly distributed among various creators. When we talk about literature, when ten percent of new literature books are worth reading, a substantial portion of them may be written by similar authors.

You could expect ten percent of the works to be of good quality. Nonetheless, only a small amount out of that ten percent will be of great quality. The more time you could concentrate on the great works, the less you'll waste time on unnecessary stuff.

Always ensure that are you not blindly adopting it as a guard for a particular area. Sturgeon's law could be valuable in a few scenarios. However, always mention it in a manner, which explains what makes it valuable. That will prevent depending on misleading reasoning.

Chapter 20: Parkinson's Law

"The work multiplies to fill the time that is accessible for its accomplishment." That is the adage of the Parkinson's Law, indicating that the more time you consume to a particular activity, the longer it will take to finish it. That's true even if you could've gotten the activity finished in a shorter time.

If you have one week to do a task, which could take you a day to finish, you'll end up extending your performance of that activity, until it brings you a week to finish it. This law has vital effects in different situations. It could have an impact on boosting your own productivity and predicting other individual's behavior.

What is included in Parkinson's Law?

The occurrence described by this law has been perceived in different scientific research. It tells that when individuals are given further time to finish a certain task, they'll take advantage of it, although they don't need it really. That doesn't result in an improved presentation on the job.

What's more, that implication often extends to further attempts to do a similar activity. When somebody is allowed further time to do a task the first time, it'll take slower than needed to finish the task in the end.

What this research tells is when individuals are given an activity to do, they think of *"how much time do I need to finish it?"* They do not consider how much time they need to finish it. That type of standpoint causes individuals to waste their time by working inefficiently.

Real Life Examples of Parkinson's Law

No matter if you're aware of it or not, you have already encountered Parkinson's law many times in your life. Below are some real life examples of this principle:

1. All year you are aware that you had a beach vacation or wedding vacation to get prepared. However, you put off healthy eating and exercise and went on a crash diet 4 weeks before your travel.

2. You had all week to finish the proposal, but you waited to finish it until 5:30 PM on Friday.

3. You had all whole semester to write your paper. However, you wrote it within the last 48 hours before the deadline. You sent it in at 4 AM in the morning it was due.

Have you experienced any of those situations? If so, you are aware of what we are talking about here. For weeks or months on end, you are paralyzed and not capable of working. Then, you suddenly become a engine during the last week before a job has to be completed.

The Origins of Parkinson's Law

Cyril Parkinson is a British historian who observed the trend through his time, along with the British Civil Service. Cyril explained that as bureaucracies lengthened, they became more incompetent and unproductive. He also applied this reflection to different other scenarios. They realize that as the size of something raised, its effectiveness lowered.

Cyril discovered that even a collection of easy activities raised in difficulty to load the time assigned to it. The job becomes easier and simpler to fix as the length of time assigned to an activity became shorter.

The principle goes hand in hand with the conviction that you need to work very hard. That kind of thinking is mirrored in the fact that managers often reward employees for hours instead of hours spent working or outcomes generated.

Parkinson's Law as a Productivity Tool

How can you take advantage of Parkinson's Law in your own work? Begin every job by determining its scope. You could try to identify how much time it will take to finish it.

Don't ask how much time you need to finish the job. As an alternative, ask yourself how much time it must take you to finish that job. Do all your best to finish the work in that given timeframe.

But how can you achieve it? You can achieve that by employing simulated time restraints. The study tells that it could result in higher outputs. Every restraint will apply to a particular job. For instance, you might utilize a timer for those short-term activities. You might prefer to use a date-based deadline for those long-term activities.

It's okay if you result in noticing that more time is needed. Nevertheless, try to finish the job before the allocated time runs out. Make sure you do it without compromising the worth of the effort. When you do this, you guarantee you don't fall into the trap of using the added time you have even if you don't really need it at all. In case you require less time than you initially thought, you can try to complete the job ahead of time. Do not allow it to drag you on.

More Uses of Parkinson's Law

The scenarios you noticed so far are emphasized under the framework of how much time you must use on chores. However, the same deliberations apply to other resources like effort and money. That denotes you must not pour resources into particular activity only because they are accessible.

Do you want to prevent this downside? Ask yourself first what advantageous results you could assume to get for the assets you wish to invest. Ensure the proportion between results-gained to resources-utilized is sufficient.

Are you thinking how much time you must spend on a particular activity? Your objective is to understand what resources you need to finish the task. Ask yourself that question instead of taking advantage of the resources you have, even if they're not needed.

Take note that Parkinson's Law helps you engage more efficiently along with other individuals. You can employ the strategies you read here to set goals and restrictions in cooperative work. Make sure that the flow of your work is as effective as possible.

What You Need to Remember

There's an important thing you need to take note of Parkinson's law. When selecting how much time or resources to dedicate to a job, pick an amount that ensures you do not waste anything unnecessarily. Make sure you also do not compromise the value of your effort.

Concentrate on setting realistic time constraints when accounting this principle. Ensure you follow by them as much as possible. That's as opposed to performing stuff like setting fewer time constraints that will ensure you don't spend excessive time on every job, leading to inferior work.

For instance, you are aware that a particular task takes at least ten minutes to finish. Knowing that will allow you to finish the task within two minutes without cramming and still do a wonderful job. Your aim here must be to determine that it takes at least ten minutes to finish the job. You need to set that time as your time limit, avoiding yourself by wasting thirty minutes on it only because you can.

Chapter 21: Useful Thinking Tools

Critical thinking is a vital ability, which moves a person from concrete ideas to abstract and conditional ideas. Critical thinking enables you to assess results, compare insights, determine parallels, order events, create information, and pull conclusions from a body of knowledge.

No matter if it's the evidence behind a math formula or an implied tone in your essay, critical thinking allows you to solve topics in real-world. You can try the following thinking tools to establish the critical thinking skills needed for success.

1. Mind Mapping

   Did you know that mind mapping is considered the small black dress of idea generation? It doesn't lose its style. In fact, it would feel wrong to walk into a company and not notice some type of mind map on a whiteboard anywhere.

   The key to mind mapping is to remember each idea, which comes up. Do not ignore anything; however far-fetch it might look. You must save all the crucial selection procedure later on. Produce as many ideas as possible. Simply put, the more ideas you write, the higher the chance of getting that golden ticket idea.

2. Get up and Get Out

Individuals often undervalue the worth of being bored. When you work around the screens throughout the day, it could prove both pleasing and comforting to get up and walk for a bit. You must allow your mind to roam around rather than concentrating on a task so difficult, it hurts you.

Why don't you walk around your local woods? Pamper yourself in your own personal contemplation montage as you skin stuns across a phone. Allow the magic of nature and the short moment of what is hopefully serene and peace, motivate and invigorate you.

A lot of people think that the practice of meditation is a wonderful way to help initiate creativity. Allow yourself to be a deep peace. You will notice how individuals might find it very soothing.

3. Adjust your Point of View

It could be difficult to achieve. However, try to position yourself in other's shoes. Often, you could be too connected to your work. Yes, and we always do it. You might be too close to see some errors that are evident from afar.

You can start sharing your ideas along with other people. Get a new pair of eyes to check at your work. Start to support constructive criticism. There's no need for you to take it all on board. It might provide up practical and helpful observations.

4. Picture Association

Are you stuck for any ideas? You can do an image search on your subject of choice. Select a random image. Work backward from the image, and you will create a story around how the image was taken.

For instance, you notice an image of a cat gazing up at the night sky. You can ask yourself what the cat could be thinking it its mind. Is it a stargazing cat? Does that cat furtively long to be an astronomer? Maybe a story about a space cat would be amazing. A space cat would make a wonderful mascot for any business.

5. Random Word Generation

This thinking tool is very simple. You only need to choose two random words and try to connect your content to it imaginatively. Basic as that.

The fun part here is how you pick to come up with the phrases and words. You could utilize an online generator tool. You can riffle through a dictionary, or you could write some words on some plastic balls. Then select the words on the first two balls you catch.

6. Lateral Thinking

This thinking tool is invented by <u>Dr. de Bono</u> that involves thinking in your scenario differently. The easiest answer isn't always correct. You resolve the majority of the problems in a linear way. For example, when something takes place, it should have... because of...

You take the step-by-step method of seeking your answers. Dr. de Bono supports other individuals to view their situation differently. Step sideways for a moment if you would. Doing this enables you to re-assess your predicament from a more creative standpoint.

For instance, you have customers who sell tractors. Are you thinking, linearly? If so, you might feel the necessity to write content about how excellent tractors are, as you need to sell tractors. Thinking about stuff, laterally opens up a new world of possibilities. You must try to look at the big picture.

What's more, tractors are a vital component to resources; farming produces food and farming as general. Take note that farms are house animals as well. A sought-after children's rhyme about farm animals is the Old McDonald. You might think about how that rhyme came to be. Why don't you make content around the origin of that rhyme?

That's only a basic instance. However, you could notice how lateral thinking could be utilized to help motivate you.

7. Six Thinking Hats

This thinking tool is also invented by Dr. Edward de Bono during the early eighties. This famous method is now utilized by different businesses across the globe. It involves putting on a collection of metaphorical hats when making a decision. Always remember that every hat symbolizes a new direction of thinking:

- Bluet Hat – Control
- Green Hat – Creativity
- Yellow Hat – Logic
- Black Hat – Caution and Judgment
- Red Hat – Emotions
- White Hat – Facts

This thinking tool could be utilized on your own or in a group. You might find yourself wearing more than one hat. You could utilize the hats to take the ego out of the balance. They allow you to think and choose topics in a rational yet creative manner.

8. The Checklist

Young kids are extremely imaginative. Their craving, creativity, and curiosity for knowledge appear to be limitless. They always ask questions about all things on the planet. But why? That's because everything is new to their eyes.

Have you ever tried to play the *"Why"* game along with a child? If yes, you will understand what we're trying to say here. It is annoying yet amazingly informative.

Now, as you get older, you are more likely to stop asking too many questions. You accept more, as it has been explained to you before. Perhaps that's the reason why most adults are viewed as having very less imagination by younger generations.

Alex Osborn is the man who is often referred to as the father of brainstorming. He developed around seventy-five creative questions to help support ideas in his book, *"Applied Imagination."* This book is worth a read once you are acquainted of it. However, to present to you some ideas, you will find universal questions, which could be asked:

- o How?
- o What?
- o Who?

o   When?

o   Where?

o   Why?

You can ask these questions to yourself each time you make some content. The probabilities are you will come up with some interesting answers.

Chapter 22: Creative Problem Solving

Creative Problem Solving is one of those key idea generation methods. Today, it's not sufficient on its own, although better service quality is vital. Without creativity and innovation, you can't expect to accomplish long-term success at a global level.

What is Creative Problem Solving?

CPS might be described as a problem solving method, which addresses a problem creatively. The key is creative as it's not apparent. The answer must solve the confirmed issue originally with the answer being grasped freely.

In the 1950s, Alex Osborn and Dr. Sidney J. Parnes invented the Osborn-Parnes (CPS) processes of solving problems creatively. The difference between this method and several Creative Problem Solving methods is that there the usage of both divergent and convergent for thinking within the sequence of every process step.

Every stage begins with a divergent thinking. It's a broad hunt for various options. After that come convergent thinking, involving assessing and choosing.

Different Models of Creative Problem Solving

You can think of no less than 4 models when defining the Osborn-Parness process of CPS:

1. **Systematic**

   The Thinking Skills Model is a type of system along with different entry points identified by the task or scenario. The structure in this model is a contract along with your present web-like unified perception of the universe.

   It portrays the unique core of every phase of renaming. This model informs you what takes place. You might observe that the diamonds sustain. What's more, the three-core focus point unites in solid colors along with the starting point varying along with the situational prerequisite.

2. **Bubble**

   During the 1990s, the diamond figures transformed into attached bubbles. It represents behavior shifts towards meaningful and directed connectedness. Directed freedom gests broader birth. You will find three distinct phrases in the bubble model.

   This tells approval to go in not just at the initial stage, but at any stage of the procedure. The linear model features diamond shapes along with flawless edges. You will also find arrows to offer directions. The 3 bubbles in this model allow you to understand what you must do exactly.

3. Linear

In this model, each of the six phases of the CPS process is defined by a diamond shape. That shape represents diverging, generating, and first options. Then, it will be followed by a set of a refreshed focus and moving on.

Models & Stages of CPS

You will find six different levels in the Osborne-Parnes process of CPS.

- **Objective Finding**

  Identifying the goal of defining your favored output is the foundation of the CPS strategy. Often, individuals pay no attention to particular aspects of the issue, initiating the obscurement of the thought process. The individual fails to consider the big picture. Defining the objective offers a lucid concept about the issue, which facilitates the study of different potential solutions to it.

- **Fact Finding**

  Gathering information about the issue and linked data is vital for understanding the problem. You can start creating a list of core information like who and what's involved, your perceptions and assumptions, standpoints of interested parties, facts, and feelings. These might help you start the process of constructing ideas.

- **Problem Finding**

Identify potential challenges which might come about and the potential opportunities present inside of it. You can do that by utilizing the problem objective as well as the collected data. That would help you with focusing on the issue. It's very easy to shift your attention away from the goal and to have the answers to the wrong problems.

- **Idea Finding**

Recycling an answer when you encounter a problem you potentially experienced beforehand is a simple procedure. Your mind senses *conceptual blocks* which is composed of challenges like faithfulness, solidity, satisfaction, and promise. Such obstruct you from thinking creatively and creating new ideas. Therefore, you must brainstorm and identify as many potential solutions as you could.

- **Solution Finding**

What is next after you have done with having new concepts? The next thing you need to do is to evaluate them to know if they meet your requirement for success and to know if it could be implemented. You can improvise, reinforce, and choose the ideal concept. Ensure that the solutions aren't just an innovative but helpful tool. Sometimes, determination is the key solution.

- **Acceptance Finding**

  You've picked the best potential resolution, which is functional and pleases the prerequisites for success. What you need to do now is to determine your roles. Identify the best steps to use the accessible resources.

How to Use CPS in a Business Setting

Whatever the issue or need your business might be dealing with, fresh approaches and creative ideas could make the difference. It provides a way to introduce change into an organization, which lowers the normal fear, which accompanies change. What's more, the process of creative problem solving turns out to be a change agent. It could convert resistance into action.

Perceiving a Problem as a Chance

One of the vital features of the CPS process is that it converts a problem into a change to enhance the company. The creative approach supports individuals to participate in a dynamic environment that supports new approaches and ideas. You can do that rather than depending on conventional ideas or past practices to fix a problem.

The reality is that the majority of organizations have the creative ability in their own environment among the staff. That creative procedure brings together different individuals. It includes line workers, office personnel, managers, supervisors, and so much more. The individuals selected to participate varies on the problem being fixed.

The creative procedure also follows a format that brings the group up to the time when creative thinking is uncovered. In the preliminary stages, the procedure achieves the following:

- Concentrates on how to sell the creative concept
- Establishes criteria for selecting ideas
- Supports participants
- Develops goals
- Determines the problem traditionally

Famous creative problem solving methods that have been established include mind mapping, brainstorming, or team game playing. The aim is to nurture individuals to feel at ease to generate ideas freely without the anxiety of disapprovals.

The Path of Creativity

In both mind mapping and brainstorming, concepts are recommended that may or may not appear sensible on the surface. However, no concept is removed, and every idea is acknowledged. One concept is associated with or mapped with other ideas. Path of ideas results to one or more creative solutions to a concern. The solution picked varies on the criteria developed at the start of the procedure.

In CPS, members of the organization are supported to join. The procedure offers acknowledgment to the individuals who are the main contributors to the success of the business. It supports positive energy, creative approaches, collaboration, as well as teamwork. Nonetheless, the most vital success factor in CPS is making sure time is committed to the creative process.

Conclusion

You will find different reasons for conflict. However, they could be distilled into the reality that everyone has unique mental models of how the world works. Such mental models are both efficient and inefficient. However, they are extremely useful in the way that they streamline everyone's lives. It also saves you the energy of having to rethink every single standpoint you have whenever you're confronted with a situation.

These mental models are all contextual. You have different models for every facet of life, from whom you decide to be friends with, to what type of music you listen to, to the types of food you and the model of the car you drive.

Now, let me ask you a question: what is your mental model? Which of these mental models are effective for you? Is it helping you? In what way?